THE WORLD OF FRANK RICHARDS

THE WORLD OF
FRANK RICHARDS

W.O.G. Lofts
&
D.J. Adley

HOWARD BAKER
LONDON

THE WORLD OF FRANK RICHARDS
W.O.G. Lofts & D.J. Adley

©Copyright: W. Lofts–D. Adley–H. Baker

First published by Howard Baker Press Limited, 1975

ISBN 0-7030-0068-3

A HOWARD BAKER BOOK

Published by Howard Baker Press Ltd.,
27a Arterberry Road, Wimbledon, London S.W.20
Typesetting by Gyro Repro of Maidstone, Kent
Printed in Great Britain by
Per Fas Printers Limited, Croydon, Surrey.

CONTENTS

FOREWORD

Since the death in 1961 of the man known to millions of readers worldwide as Frank Richards, there have been many attempts to write his biography.

Unfortunately, until now, no such book has been published. Which is a great pity. One cannot read enough about the man who gave such pleasure to so many generations of readers.

But producing such a book is far from easy, as we have discovered. Indeed, when Howard Baker suggested that we attempt an authoritative life of our favourite author what seemed at first sight to be a straightforward matter of simply assembling a series of facts proved, in practice, to be a most difficult task.

Frank Richards' famous characters have been analysed in a hundred different ways and discussed times without number. The history of *The Magnet* and of *The Gem* has been dealt with exhaustively. Thousands of articles in every kind of publication from *Horizon* to *Titbits* have touched on the Frank Richards stories, and one does not want to keep on going over the same old ground. To add something new to the mountain of extant material on Frank the man turned out to be harder.

Clearly Frank Richards went out of his way to avoid

shedding anything but the smallest glimmer of light upon his personal life. His Autobiography — which should have been a mine of fascinating fact — succeeded only in leaving its subject more shadowy than ever.

Plainly he wished to keep his private life private, and this desire was respected during his lifetime. There are still a few people today who feel that the subject should remain taboo, but with this we cannot agree. Frank Richards is history now, and history cannot be suppressed. Attempted suppression leads only, more often than not, to an unwelcome distortion of the facts.

It is this, particularly, we seek to avoid.

To all those who have helped us in this work, our sincere thanks. Some acknowledgements will be found in the following pages, but others must be made here to that great 'band of brothers' — The Directors, editors, sub-editors and other workers of the old Amalgamated Press — many of whom have become our personal friends down the years. Especially must we acknowledge the help given us by the late Mr. C.M. Down, *The Magnet* editor who revealed to us many hitherto unknown facts about the paper.

But the picture we paint in these pages, and responsibility for it, is ours alone.

It is as near a true, lifelike portrait of Frank Richards as we are, at the present time, able to make it.

W.O.G. Lofts
D.J. Adley
1975

CHAPTER ONE

the early world of Frank Richards

Snow, thicker and thicker, the white flakes were falling incessantly. . .

Snow had been falling all the night, and the park gleamed white as Wharton and Hurree Singh tramped towards the frozen lake.

Billy Bunter was a guest of sorts at Wharton Lodge for the Christmas Holidays. . .

Christmas is a golden time, a glowing time, a time for festivities and renewing acquaintanceships with old friends. And what better friends could one have than those who are to be found in the pages of *The Magnet* and *Gem*?

The wonderful stories featuring Billy Bunter, Harry Wharton & Co. of Greyfriars, along with Arthur Augustus D'Arcy and Tom Merry & Co of St. Jims are often re-read avidly at Christmastide, for they bring back nostalgic memories of the past when Christmas was a truly festive occasion.

So what a sense of loss there must have been in innumerable homes — what a wave of sadness — when, on Boxing Day 1961, the BBC announced that the creator of all these imperishable stories had died at his home at Kingsgate, Kent, on Christmas Eve, aged eighty-six.

For countless thousands it was the death of a very real friend.

How ironic it was that he should depart this life on the very eve of the day that he wrote of so well. For Frank Richards loved Christmas, particularly the old-fashioned kind.

In the Christmas stories of Greyfriars the scene was set more often than not at Wharton Lodge, with Wells the butler, and Colonel and Amy Wharton. There would be a blazing log fire in the Hall, holly and mistletoe and paper-chains. For dinner roast turkey, plum puddings, mince pies and crackers with all the traditional trimmings. And this, of course, against a backdrop of frosted windowpanes and endlessly falling thick, fleecy white snow beyond.

Sometimes, in dead of winter's night, there might be a ghost for good measure: clanking chains and eerie footsteps, secret panels and hidden staircases. Or the scene might be shifted to Cavendale Abbey, Mauleverer Towers, Reynham Castle (or Eastwood House in the *Gem.*) But of all Christmas holiday locations, Wharton Lodge was clearly the firm favourite of successive generations of readers.

And now the man who had held those generations in thrall with the power of his pen, the man known to the world as Frank Richards, the man who had so long used this name that it had almost replaced his real name of Charles Hamilton, this man — at last — had passed on.

It is one of the oddities of Frank Richards' life that personal fame lagged far behind achievement. Although he enjoyed enormous publicity before his death — more than any other boys' author past or present — until the early forties he was recognized by only a few staff members at Fleetway House. To everyone else, he was but a pen-name or rather a series, a collection of pen-names.

When the limelight finally began to beat on him, Frank Richards was rising seventy, and the mists of time had long since shrouded his boyhood. Those who had an inkling of the truth, and those who were tempted to delve, alike refrained from public comment, as they were reluctant to offend an old and honoured writer.

As always, the main result of a suppression of facts was a flowering of speculation. What particularly stimulated curiosity was that the man who for half a century had been the world's most prolific author for boys, and who had reached his highest fame through school stories which were held in affectionate memory by millions, was mute on the subject of his own boyhood. It was certainly odd.

When Frank Richards steps out of page one of his own Autobiography he is already seventeen and has found his vocation in writing. Where was he born? one may well ask. Who were his parents? What school did he attend? And did he draw upon his experiences there for his fascinating pen pictures of life at Greyfriars and St. Jim's?

Was he happy, or miserable? A scholar, or dunce? And — drop your voice to a whisper! — was he ever one of those gay blades who smoked a surreptitious Woodbine or invested a speculative tanner with the local bookie?

Not one word does he tell us. As a result, conjecture has long enjoyed free rein among the interested, and some widely varying views have resulted.

One of these was that he must have been at Harrow — presumably with no better foundation than that he was acquainted with *Forty Years On*! Others who noted his aptness for publicity in later life concluded, with more reason, that snobbery dictated the self-imposed silence about his youth. A final uncharitable few supposed that he must have had something positively detrimental to hide.

In the main, however, his reticence was respected. People believed that the truth could be unearthed, and that his obituary notices would dispel the mystery in the end.

But, as it happened, they didn't. Fleet Street, for once, was as ignorant as its readers, and the speculator was left to put his own construction on just three relevant sentences — the only relevant sentences contained in all of Frank Richards' writing:

"As a very small boy I secretly and surreptitiously taught myself the Greek Alphabet, in the happy delusion that it would prove the Open Sesame to my father's mysterious books."

"True, as a boy I wrote reams and reams sprawling in my old boat on summer days."

"[When a boy] I saw myself translating the Iliad ever so much more attractively than Pope or Chapman."

Just these three hints. Nothing more.

The wide publicity afforded his death and, later, the publication of his will, naturally contained many references to this reserve, and various statements made at the time by relatives did little to dispel the fog. In fact, as family, they merely confirmed the assumption that Frank's father was of Scots descent, that his mother came from a well-to-do land-owning family in Oxfordshire, and that the family originally hailed from Chiswick.

Subsequently in an interview, Frank Richards' one surviving sister, Mrs Una Harrison, was able to shed more light. The last of eight brothers and sisters, she was a small, charming and cultured lady with a great sense of humour. A talented musician, she had passed every examination she attempted with high honours before becoming a teacher of music. She had married a musician and composer, the late Percy Harrison, who collaborated with Frank Richards in the football song *On the Ball* popular about 1914-18 and, by the strangest coincidence, a ditty which the Greyfriars and St. Jim's juniors insisted on singing on the slightest provocation!

Then entering her eighties, Mrs Harrison was unfortunately at some disadvantage in attempting to recall the early background of her family. Apart from the natural difficulty in casting one's mind back so far, she was six years Frank's junior. She had not known her grandparents and her father died when she was only two.

Her earliest recollection of childhood days was of the family living in the Chiswick area and of brother Charles — the young Frank Richards — attending a school for Young Gentlemen. She recalled visits with her mother to well-to-do relatives who lived in Oxfordshire, and it was assumed quite rightly that her mother's family had its roots in that country. The surname of Hamilton presupposed that, on their father's side, the family was of Scots descent, with hints of affinity with the Dukes of Hamilton. A Scots connection there almost certainly was, as one of her brothers once had a large claymore which had been handed down for generations as a family heirloom.

Near Ealing Broadway is a part of the town that, at the time of Frank Richards' death, was hardly affected by modern development. In a maze of lanes just off one of the earliest main roads in the former County of Middlesex was a turning named Oak Street. This consisted of a row of very old two-storey cottages which had undergone some modern-isation. It was in the one numbered 15 that any biography of Frank Richards really begins for it was here that he first saw the light of day on the 8th August, 1876. He was the sixth child, christened Charles Harold St. John Hamilton.[1]

As late as 1963, one's impressions of Oak Street could well be likened to those of television's Coronation Street, for the two looked much alike. Number 15 had lately been fitted with a new, pale lemon coloured front door. But most unusual was a lamp-post, only a foot away from the house in the tiny cemented area that represented the front garden. An ordinary everyday lamp-post. It had been there for as far back as the tenant at that time could remember — which was at least forty years.

Why a lamp post should be erected in such a peculiar position is a mystery, unless the house had formerly opened straight onto the street with no area or front garden intervening. The tenant could suggest no other solution, and the name of Hamilton meant nothing to him. But this last, of course, was only to be expected, since the Hamiltons had moved from this address at least seventy-eight years pre-viously.

And now the house itself has gone, to make way for the modern development which in 1962 was fast overtaking it. On the whole, the house and Oak Street itself were both unimpressive. At best, in 1962, they could only be said to be

1 His brothers and sisters were Maud Marion Margaret (1865), Edith Hilda May (1872), Una Isabel Gertrude (1881), Alexander Llewellyn Patrick (1867), Archibald Reginald Percy (1869), Richard Lionel Walter (1874) and Hugh Douglas Percy (1879).

dingy, dull and respectable. But in 1876, one can imagine, this would have been a smart and pretty little lower middle-class street.

Much the same can be said of Lancaster Road, Charles Hamilton's second home. Next door to the house where he lived was Ealing British Schools, which it is thought he at one time attended in company with his brothers. But he actually began his schooling at a Church School, and soon entered into the mysteries of the "three r's" under the delightful classification of 'Mixed Infant'.

Before leaving the subject of Hamilton's birthplace there are two other items worthy of interest. The first is that within two minutes' walk of this typically Victorian back-water one was suddenly plunged into a thoroughly modern and up-to-date area of West London, all garish neon and brilliantly lit supermarkets. It was as though the calendar had been suddenly accelerated by three quarters of a century.

The second point worth mentioning is that only a short walk away from Oak Street is a well-to-do thoroughfare where stood the home of another prolific writer for boys, the late H.H. Clifford Gibbons, better known as 'Gilbert Chester' the Sexton Blake author. What is remarkable about this is that the name of the thoroughfare is Hamilton Road!

Charles's mother, Mrs Mary Ann Hannah Hamilton, was born on the 7th June 1847 at Townsend Road, St John's Wood, but came from a St Marylebone family and was one of thirteen children.

Her father, Stephen T.B. Trinder, who seems to have been something of a local character, was a fly-driver (a sort of cabby) who branched out into nearly as many business ventures as Fisher T. Fish. He became an agent for both the Ealing fly-drivers and Scottish Union Insurance, a licensed broker and appraiser, a bailiff, an estate agent and a house valuer.

His wife shared his enterprising spirit and in addition to rearing her brood of thirteen children ran a highly successful second-hand clothing business. After her death it was carried

Top: OAK STREET
Bottom: The house where "Frank Richards" was born.
Photo's: Copyright. Trevor Adley

EVERY TUESDAY

THE Magnet LIBRARY

A Complete Story-Book, attractive to all Readers.

ONE HALFPENNY

The New Term at Greyfriars

A Splendid, Long, Complete School Tale of Harry Wharton & Co.
By FRANK RICHARDS.

THE FIRST CHAPTER.
Back to School!

THERE were faces at all the windows in the train, and a deafening din proceeding from most of the carriages. The express swept on through a snowy landscape, leaving a trail of black smoke and an echo of shouting voices behind.

The boys of Greyfriars were returning to school after the Christmas vacation. The special train was crammed from end to end, and, although by no means glad that the holidays were over, the trainload of youthful humanity seemed in high enough spirits, and they were celebrating their return to the old school in the most vociferous way possible.

From one carriage especially the din was terrific. It was a carriage occupied by fellows belonging to the Remove, the Lower Fourth Form. The Removites of Greyfriars generally made their presence heard wherever they were, but on the present occasion they were excelling all previous efforts.

The carriage was crammed: every seat was taken, and fellows were standing at the windows or sitting on one another's knees. Frank Nugent was playing the "Grand March" from "Tannhauser" on his mouth organ. The effect, from a musical point of view, was somewhat spoiled by the fact that Bob Cherry was playing "Bill Bailey" on a tin whistle at the same time. Bulstrode, Skinner, and Stott were telling some unknown person, at the full force of their lungs, to love them and the world was theirs. Wun Lung, the Chinese boy, was singing a song in Chinese, which had an apparently endless refrain of "Ko, ke, ko, ke, ko, ko, ke!"—or something that sounded like that. Hurree Jamset Ram Singh, the Hindu junior, not to be outdone, had burst into an unintelligible chanting melody, celebrating the heroic deeds of Rama, in a language only known to himself. Harry Wharton was almost the only one who was not singing something, and he was stopping his ears.

"Hold on, you chaps!" exclaimed Nugent, suddenly breaking off his stirring march. "You're off-side! Can't you keep quiet, and listen to the music?"

"That's what we want you to do," said Bulstrode. "I wish you'd shut up that unearthly instrument. Go it, Skinny! Buck up, Stott! 'Lo-o-ve me, and the world is mi-ine!'"

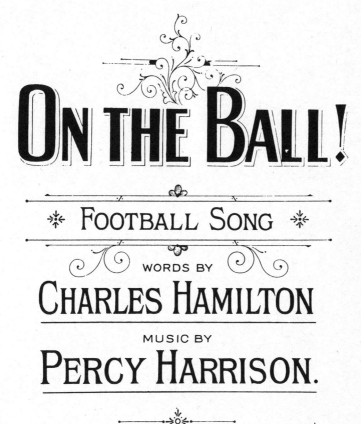

On the Ball!

FOOTBALL SONG

WORDS BY

CHARLES HAMILTON

MUSIC BY

PERCY HARRISON.

Copyright.   Price 6ᵈ net.

STANFORD & Cᵒ.
82, WELLS ST., OXFORD ST.,
LONDON, W.

A POPULAR GREYFRIARS SONG

THE VANGUARD LIBRARY.

1D/2

No. 28. PUBLISHED EVERY TUESDAY. ½d.

·BILLY·BUNTER'S·HAMPER·
·A·STORY·OF·TAFFY·LLEWELLYN'S·SCHOOLDAYS·

—(:o:)—

By H. PHILPOTT WRIGHT.

—(:o:)—

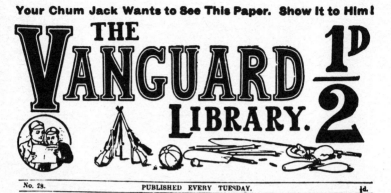

CHAPTER I.

FETCHING THE HAMPER—JONATHAN B. PANKICK TELLS OF A
MAN WITH AN APPETITE.

"HURRAH! Dear old Aunt Selina has sent me a
hamper of tuck," cried Billy Bunter, as with an open
letter in his hand he cantered up to a group of his
particular chums.

"Good old auntie! What has she sent us, Billy?" asked
Tommy Rottinger.

"Dunno, exactly, but she says she has sent me a nice large
hamper and hopes I will make judicious and careful use of the
contents."

"That sounds all right, but hasn't auntie enumerated
the articles?"

"No, you muff, of course, she hasn't," growled Billy.
"But Aunt Selina is jolly well off, and I know the hamper
will contain plenty of everything, although she has never sent
me one before. Says she's going to look after me while the
mater's away."

"Its sure to be all right, then," remarked Dicky Bird, otherwise Canary. "Now the point is, how are we going to get it
in without Sneak Tadpole or anyone else twigging it?"

"Better take it on a truck as far as Mrs. Swallowbeam's,
and then carry it to the attic in the same way that we did
Taffy's old mummy," suggested Jack Hardwick.

"That's the idea," agreed Billy.

"Has auntie addressed it to the school?" asked Ratscombe
Beynon.

"I expect so, but, of course, we must fetch it from the
station. It will never do to let it fall into the hands of the
Philistines."

"It is to be hoped our efforts to hire a truck won't be so
expensive as they were last time," observed Taffy.

"When do you expect the hamper, Billy?" queried
Jonathan B. Pankick, the boy from Colorado.

"Aunt Selina says in this letter that she despatched it
yesterday morning, so it ought to be at the station by this
afternoon.

"All right, then, all of you be good little boys so as not to
be kept in this afternoon," said Taffy.

The above conversation took place in the playground of
Blackminister School during the morning interval on the
Wednesday following the events recorded in "Bowled Out,"
the last, Taffy Llewellyn, story in this series.

In that it will be remembered, we recorded the adventures
of Taffy and Billy Bunter on their way to Paddleton Station.

The lads had since been ferretted out and interviewed
by the police, but steadfast in their resolve to maintain at all
costs the secret of the vault they had discovered, our two
friends had related only the incidents which had occurred
in the train.

Readers of No. 24 of the VANGUARD will recollect that
Taffy, by means of his great talent as a ventriloquist, had

on most capably by some of her daughters, with a branch in Church Street Market, at Paddington.

Mrs Hamilton spent her childhood in the shadow of Lords Cricket Ground and followed the example of her mother by marrying when only sixteen. The wedding was at the Congregational Church in Ealing in 1864. Charles' parents then settled down in this district, if not in any one particular home. They lived at several different addresses, including St Mary's Place where the eldest child was born, before moving to Oak Street.

The naming of Alexander Llewellyn Patrick Hamilton, this eldest boy, indicates a small revolt against the family and Victorian tradition of naming the first-born after the father, and the rather pretentious clutches of names with which all the family were endowed suggests more of a romantic than a Scottish influence.

Charles' father, John Hamilton was a Master Carpenter — formerly a stationer — whilst his grandfather, likewise a John Hamilton, does not seem to have had a formal education, but was nevertheless a clever landscape gardener.

There is no doubt that the Hamiltons could lay claim to a Scots background, and were proud of it. One ancestor is known to have fought — on the losing side — at the Battle of Culloden. Fleeing south, he settled in Berkshire where he soon acquired a thriving estate, owning amongst other property a hostelry known as the Black Horse Inn.

The family fortunes seem to have declined later on, but Charles's father, who was certainly well-educated, seems to have remade them to some extent. Generally the family could be said to be of a solid middle-class background, and John Hamilton — who was in many respects very much the Victorian papa — ruled the household with a rod of iron.

He was a careful man and an economical one. Anything that was broken was not to be thrown away but kept to be repaired with his tools and his gluepot. A clever man and a thorough craftsman he also dabbled in poetry and is likewise known to have written prose, but there is no evidence that any of his pieces was ever printed.

In fact, many years later, in a special issue of *The Magnet*

Charles rather bitterly remarked that his 'father never even received remuneration for the ink he used in writing', but certainly the flair for poetry was not wasted. It was passed on, and Charles and his sisters could all write verse with facility.

John Hamilton's unbending sternness and strictness, coupled with the fact that he was by no means a teetotaler, cast something of a cloud over the children's early days. Charles himself later related that once, when a small friend told him his father had died, he horrified his school-mate by replying: "I wish mine had."

But there is something to be pleaded in mitigation for John Hamilton.

In 1881, whilst still only 42, he developed the cancer that was to kill him three years later on 20 February 1884. Charles was only seven-and-a-half at the time of his father's death, so that during the period when the boy was at his most impressionable and least able to appreciate all of the facts, his father was suffering the mounting agonies of a fatal disease.

Although the family says that with their father's death a weight seemed to be lifted from them, new problems arose. The still youthful widow had eight children to provide for, and opportunities for women to follow gainful employment were not as plentiful in those days as they are now. For a short time, Mrs Hamilton met her difficulties by carrying on a second-hand clothing business — the same trade in which her mother and several of her sisters were already engaged — and notices to this effect can be seen in the advertisement columns of *The Middlesex Times* for 1884. The business was run from the house in Lancaster Road, next door to the Ealing British Schools, but this did not continue for long.

Soon, Mrs Hamilton's young brother, the influential Walter Trinder, stepped in to put the family finances on a sound footing, and the Hamiltons moved to what the house agents describe as the more 'socially desirable' district of Chiswick.

And it was now, too, that money was found to invest in the boys' education. Alex, the eldest son, had left school at fourteen, but Charles and Richard were sent to a 'School for

Young Gentlemen'.

THORN HOUSE SCHOOL, EALING
H.P. GREAVES, ESQ
Principal

French, German, Latin Greek and English taught.
Teacher of Modern Languages.
Dr. G. Von Cronenthall

Upper and Lower Classical and Modern
Sides. The Lower School consists of
the Upper and Lower First and Upper
and Lower Second Forms.

Fees: Day Scholar £3.3.0 per term
Upper School £5.5.0 per term

One clue which led to the discovery of this school was dropped by W.E. Stanton-Hope in a Fleet Street pub, a gathering place for old editors of Fleetway House. While editing the comic paper *Chuckles* he himself had been a great friend of Charles Hamilton.

Hope, an established writer himself, related how he once received a letter from a Greek publisher, which was all very flattering — but there was a snag. Hope couldn't read it, for it was written in Classical Greek, a language which he had not mastered.

Meeting Charles Hamilton shortly afterwards, he asked him to translate it for him, and subsequently congratulated him upon the speed and facility with which he executed the task.

"My old language teacher, Doctor Von Cronenthall, would have been pleased to hear that," was Hamilton's rejoinder and, because it was so unusual to hear him mention anything of his early life, Hope had never forgotten it.

Some years later another clue fell. Charles Maurice Down, editor of *The Magnet* and *Gem* related how once, in a discussion on the subject of the fictional seats of learning that he had created, Hamilton had revealed that Rookwood, with its Classical and Modern Sides, was identical in many ways to the school he had himself attended. So it was Thorn House!

Thorn House and Rookwood were both divided into Classical and Modern Sides, but what other features they shared is now impossible to determine. For, contrary to Charles Hamilton's belief in the persistence of memory, time has erased every local recollection of the school and even the building has disappeared.

All that remains is the entry already quoted in a contemporary directory of private schools, and whether this is included on merit or simply because of the Principal's willingness to pay for listing is also unknown, but it would be nice to believe merit the cause. Certainly whilst Mr Greaves makes no mention of any degree qualification of his own, the Modern Language section looks very impressive under the heading of a conjoint doctorate and an aristocratic particle!

Remarkable as it may seem, only one descendant still remains from the original family of eight brothers and sisters. This is Mrs Una Hamilton Wright, Charles' niece, the daughter of Mrs Una Harrison who died suddenly in 1963.

Mrs Wright, who lives in the Midlands and is well known for her charitable, hospital and social work, has proved most friendly and co-operative. Above all, she is a mine of information about her favourite 'Uncle Charlie'.

As might be expected, she reveals that he was a voracious reader as a boy and when only eleven learned the whole of *The Lay of the Last Minstrel* by heart for no other reason save that he liked it.

In contrast, he was also passionately fond of Wild West stories, then much in vogue, and he read them avidly. When he had run out of printed material he would invent his own Western yarns and then create a fictional farm in Canada. It was his own special farm with a representative of every species of animal on it. Nothing at all was excluded and many exciting things happened there which he would describe to his brothers and sisters. The interesting point that emerges, of course, is that even when quite young his imagination was equal to anything demanded of it.

That same imagination could on occasion make life a little disquieting for his younger brother and sister when they played their favourite game of 'Burglars' — a sort of home-made nineteenth century 'Murder'.

It was a night-time game, and the idea was to rush upstairs in the dark armed with a poker and rattle the weapon on the empty grate of each of the bedrooms at the top of the house, hoping to produce in the other children a tantalising tingle of fright. For it was always just remotely possible that there *was* somebody there.

But Charles used to make their blood curdle with terror.

He could make the most eerie frightening noises. So much so that the little ones would be sure there *was* an intruder and would hurtle downstairs, petrified, to land in a heap on the hall floor.

There were certain tasks that his imagination could not tackle, however. One of them was mathematics in any shape or form. He used to say that he was simply incapable of adding up a column of figures and getting it right, and that if he were to add it up more than once he would get a different answer each time.

One of the earliest luxuries he afforded himself was 'somebody to sort the figures out'. For this reason Income Tax and Supertax were always malevolent mysteries to him. Perhaps this explains why he delighted in gambling when on the Continent — it was all a matter of luck whether the numbers were for you or against you, no matter whether they were numbers on a roulette wheel, the figures in a tax return, or arithmetical exercises in a schoolbook.

Charles's love of literature and languages showed itself very early in life. For as Mrs Wright reports, "Very early his predilection for Latin showed itself and he soon discovered that his Latin master was only one chapter ahead of the class in Kennedy's primer. So he took it upon himself to get two chapters ahead and catch the master out with an awkward question for which he was not prepared."

When asked about his schooldays, Charles Hamilton would reply that he was like the man in *Who's Who* who entered his school as Eton as his education as 'self'. For fear of hurting the feelings of old friends he would decline to specify which school it was that he had attended, as many of his characters no doubt owed some of their traits to his classmates and teachers.

But the master already described was clearly one who would find no delight in discussing Sophocles with his Head. So those seeking a model for Mr Quelch will have to look further afield than Thorn House, where the Latin master was only one jump ahead of the First Form in the primer.

It appears, then, that whatever the relevance or irrelevance of Eton there is much to be said for the 'self-education'. Certainly education and schooling are not synonymous and any deficiencies in Thorn House or its curriculum would be rectified in time by Charles Hamilton's naturally studious nature.

In his mature opinion, Richards believed that school should be a place for making the acquaintance of the greatest minds of our civilisation, not for hard grinding at indigestible facts for examination purposes. He saw education as an enlargement of one's knowledge of people and their thinking processes, not as a cramming course.

As a boy Charles was small and slight, physical characteristics which were to remain with him for life. In his mental processes, too, the child was very much the father of the man: diffident and withdrawn.

His brother, Dick, two years older but in the same class, used to include him in his own group of bigger boys as a sort of favour, and he was known as 'Dick's young brother' who could be counted on to offer an intelligent suggestion when required and to shut up in the meantime.

Dick was very gregarious and always had a gang of boys about him, but Charles would dodge them if he could do so politely and find a quiet spot to read a book. Not, he hastened to explain, because he didn't like Dick's friends, but because he found people in books more interesting company.

Our author mentioned many times that he drew his own boyish self-portrait in Frank Nugent of the Greyfriars Remove. A word of caution here. The reader who meets Nugent first, and most logically, in No. 1 of The Magnet in

1908 will find him a boy mighty with fists and feet. Clearly the self-portraiture did not begin until Nugent had dwindled somewhat in stature, status and athleticism.

Once developed into a true and consistent character, Frank Nugent appears as a somewhat unobtrusive and unassertive boy. Physically the least impressive of the Famous Five, he teeters on the brink of inclusion in the football and cricket elevens but rarely squeezes in save when the ranks are depleted by illness or dissension. Throughout, he bears with unusual and commendable patience and fortitude the discomforts of Harry Wharton's uncertain temper and often stiff-necked pride.

He is no Hero with a capital aitch, but his quietly attractive personality rounds off the group of the five leading juniors and gives it an artistic unity which would have been marred by the inclusion of a more self-assertive and would-be dominant figure.

Thus, allowing for the fettling and polishing inevitable in fiction, the broad outlines of similarity between the two boys are clearly visible.

Charles, who was nicknamed 'Bags' by his family because of some incident connected with his first or second breeching, was noted for his courtesy and politeness at an age when most of us present little polish but many rough edges. As one of a group of boys at school he was never the leader, but was always popular as a trusty follower, ever willing to do odd jobs and stooge for those who planned the schoolboy exploits.

Hints and surmises that he may have spent some time in Canada — thus bringing an element of truth into the stories of Cedar Creek (*Boys Friend Weekly* 'Frank Richards Schooldays' 1917) — are unfounded, as he had never in his life visited the land of the Mounties. When asked about this his evasive reply was that 'it is possible the tales were influenced by my own schooldays'. But he always refused to say when he had visited Canada, or which part.

Certainly as a boy we wrote reams and reams, sprawling in an old boat on summer days on the Thames near Chiswick and one knows that this is the essence of Frank Richards, the storyteller supreme.

Known as 'Charlie the peacemaker' he could not bear arguments and quarrels, was well-known to be polite and courteous and all his life set a high value on good manners. He was never known to lose his temper. He valued the gift of life very highly and hated to see people wasting their lives and their opportunities. All in all, he simply set out to be a thoroughly good boy.

When he finally left Thorn House his education was continued by a private tutor. This highly cultured elderly lady taught him Italian and polished up his Latin. She became a friend of the family and Charles enjoyed an intellectual companionship with her for many years.

But this lay in the future. Right now Charles Hamilton was seventeen years of age and just about to embark on his career in the world of boys' literature.

CHAPTER TWO

the foundations

The Friardale cobbler turned to his son. There was emotion in his strong, thoughtful face. "Dick, my boy, I'm going," said Mr. Penfold. "Goodbye, Dick, and remember your mother and me are thinking of you all the time." Dick's eyes were moist. "I'm not likely to forget that, father." "No, I don't think you are, Dick, and if you get on in this 'ere school, Dick, and rise above your own trade, you ain't likely to be ashamed of the folks, I know!"

BY SHEER GRIT! *The Magnet*
No. 194, 28th October 1911

Thus Dick Penfold entered a new world, a station far above his own, and in some respects his position could be likened to that of Charles Hamilton upon leaving school.

But in Hamilton's case the step was taken not as any kind of a path up the social ladder but purely to advance himself in his chosen profession. For we may rely upon it that he had long since decided what he was going to do with his life.

The strange thing is that in doing it, and in doing it so well, he virtually lost his own identity. In his autobiography he even writes of his alter ego as a separate and distinct person.

"Frank Richards at seventeen —" he begins "— was at a loose end. He was in the perplexing state of not knowing what he was going to do."

We do not have to believe it.

The die had almost certainly been cast in his earlier scribbling days. Now resolution strengthened ambition, and it was at the age of seventeen, in the year 1894, that he had his first story accepted for publication.

The writing phenomenon later known to the world as Frank Richards was born.

If he can be said to have demonstrated any subject specialisation in these days it must have been for sea stories, then very popular, but which now seem to have completely fallen from favour. He wrote many of them. In fact, prolific as he was in almost every sort of story then featured in boys' weeklies, adventure yarns accounted for a considerable part of his total output. But had he remained a 'general practitioner' he would also have remained just another boys' writer in the ranks of that faceless army which fed the insatiable popular presses of the day.

It was time for a change.

Frank Richards possessed an excellent sense of timing. Consider his birth — a piece of astonishing luck. Had it been delayed twenty years the golden opportunity of *The Gem* and *The Magnet* would never have come his way. Had it been advanced twenty, he could not have dreamed of becoming a specialist writer of school stories: such a thing would have been impossible. More than this — no matter what his gifts and inclinations he would not have been able to make a living out of writing boys' fiction alone.

Open any issue of a boys' paper between 1860 and 1890 and work by a handful of perennial favourites will be found. Percy Bollinbroke St John and his brother Vane Ireton St John (which look like exceptionally pretentious pen-names but were not), Bracebridge Hemyng, Charles Stevens, James Greenwood, Edwin Harcourt Burrage and George Emmett — all were as prolific as Frank Richards and probably no less talented.

They were in unfailing demand. They rang the changes on pirates, highwaymen, school, historical and adventure stories but still they could not follow their natural bent completely. An equally natural urge to eat compelled them to eke out their incomes writing for penny-dreadfuls or doing catch-penny editorial work. They could not specialise.

Frank Richards arrived on the scene when the 1870 Education Act was beginning to effectively improve the literacy of the great mass of the population. Determined to write, and with the assistance of a relative he made his first contact with a publisher. In his autobiography Frank Richards was intentionally mysterious and called this gentle-man "Mr M", though for what reason is not clear.

Dowling Maitland was far from being a mysterious fellow, and not at all like the 'M' of James Bond novels and films. Editor and agent-cum-author he seemingly had his finger in almost every contemporary literary pie. At the time Frank Richards met him he was looking for new authors and also had an idea for starting a new boys' paper. Straight-way, on meeting, he remarked how very young Frank Richards looked, and one is not surprised. Small, frail, and a boyish seventeen 'M' no doubt wondered why he was not at school. However, an agreement struck, the rewarding outcome was a cheque for five guineas duly received by Frank Richards in the post.

As he revealed later, despite the many thousands of cheques he received in the years to come, the majority of which were for much larger sums, this particular cheque gave him his greatest thrill.[1]

'M' alas soon cut him down to proper size again if he felt six feet tall after receiving that payment, for he reduced his rates for future stories.

Having established himself in the world of fiction Frank Richards' enthusiasm grew and he set about the task of becoming a writer to be read and appreciated. But public-ation, though regular, was slow for this youngster and he had yet to find his market. A number of his pieces were accepted

---

1 This was not the first money he had earned with his pen. The first payment he ever received was for an article; the sum, twelve shillings and sixpence.

by such publishers as Brett and Roberts but, lacking a by-line these stories are now lost to posterity.

Eventually he was successful in finding a market with the fairly new company of Harmsworth Brothers, later to become The Amalgamated Press, where he was to find fame if not fortune. His earliest published stories, under the name Charles Hamilton, are all pirate yarns with such titles as *The Corsair Captain* (1895), *The Slaver Captain, Sunk at Sea,* and *Captain Nemo.*

In 1899 he made a real impact with a company that was to publish such a considerable number of his stories that he must have not only been their star writer, but obviously also had the rare distinction of having them publish everything he offered them. This company was Trapps Holmes, a firm founded by the two Georges: George Holmes and George Trapps.

It was suggested in an article published some years ago in Frank Richards' lifetime that he may have written only a few dozen stories for this publisher, but this brought the prompt reply that he had written *"not less than one thousand stories for their Smiles, Funny Cuts, Worlds Comic, Picture Fun, Vanguard and Coloured Comic."*

After a long investigation, it has been possible not only to confirm Frank Richards' statement but also to reliably estimate that the final total was several thousand stories, and that Frank Richards was being modest in the extreme.

Almost every issue of Trapps Holmes publications had a touch of Richards about it. Either his name was on a story, or a pen-name which has since been proved to be his. For a period of more than five years Frank Richards swamped these publications with work from his pen, and when one realises that these were the days before the Remington and every single word had to be written in longhand one appreciates that our author must have been writing every moment of the day and often far into the night.

H.J. Drane, the editor of Trapps Holmes, must have been amazed at Frank Richards' output and clearly made a mental note to secure his services when he started his own publishing company much later.

Most of Frank Richards' early stories were nothing but pot-boilers and would be very little interest to readers today. They covered every single theme and subject from Deadshot Dick, to policemen, firemen and gold-diggers. Curiously, he made very little impact with his school tales and he did not concentrate on them in earnest until 1905 when the Amalgamated Press ran them in the *Union Jack* and *Marvel*.

Probably the most interesting fact about his pre-Greyfriars and St Jim's stories was that almost a year before the first story of Greyfriars appeared in *The Magnet* a story was published in the comic paper, *Smiles* No. 47 (March 19th 1907) entitled *The Captain's Cure* and it was about a school called Greyfriars!

Could this have been the forerunner of the famous school we know so well? Were the boys at the school earlier inhabitants than Harry Wharton & Co? One will never know, for Frank Richards died before this discovery was made.

The story was quite amusing in its way and period, but far too short to give any depth to characterisation or plot. The principle boy was Tom Lawrence of the Lower Fourth and the two bullies of the Fifth were Lamb and Sharp. Captain of the school and Wingate's probable predecessor was a youth named Conway.

The moral was there in Frank Richards' stories, even in those days, and it was delivered without any unnecessary preaching:

> Lamb and Sharp were two Fifth-Form boys and the worst bullies of Greyfriars. They had other objectionable traits, also being suspected of smoking secretly in their studies. They also encouraged smaller boys to do the same.

Another tale of Greyfriars appeared in *Smiles* No. 59 entitled *The Cricket Captain,* in which the school played against Redclyffe and lost by an innings.

The village of Friardale has always featured prominently in the Greyfriars scene and a Friardale School appeared in Frank Richards' Trapps Holmes stories when a French master named Monsieur Mornay was the exact double of Monsieur Charpentier of Greyfriars.

From this point Frank Richards seemed to concentrate soley on school stories, and a full list of them would show the reader his astounding output in that period.

Many of the characters he employed at this time had names similar to those used much later in his more famous stories of Greyfriars and St. Jims. Some enthusiasts have remarked that it was a weakness for him to repeat characters' names but his output was so vast that he probably could not remember all the names of the characters he had used previously. To list but a few: Gore, Mr Mimble, Dick Russell, Clare, Blane, Figgins, Carne, Trimble, Dr Lascelles, Talbot (who later appeared in *Jester Comic,* an elder brother of Reginald Talbot the Toff of St Jim's) and an Indian boy named Koumi Rao — nicknamed Inky (and could have been his double) by his friends — who eventually turned up at St. Jim's in 1913.

Many stories appeared with Charles Hamilton as the author, whilst others were under a variety of pen-names.[2] Even when a story was anonymous, more often than not the initials C.H. would be found at the end of the tale.

Another curious trait was that when a story was anonymous he had the habit of always ending it with the words of the title.

Funny Cuts also featured a schoolboy detective named Sedley Sharpe, who was an obvious antecedent of Jack Drake and Len Lex, and these stories were far superior to many of his other early creations.

The year 1906 was to see the publication of the first story of one of his famous schools *Jack Blake of St. Jim's* in the Amalgamated Press paper *Pluck,* but this has so much importance that it will be dealt with separately in the next chapter.

Frank Richards always maintained that he ceased to write for Trapps Holmes as a result of persuasion by Percy Griffith, the first editor of *The Magnet* and *Gem,* but this does not seem to be the case. For although Griffith left the Amalgamated Press in 1911 stories from our author's pen were still

[2] For full list see Appendix 1.

being published by Trapps Holmes as late as 1915.

Of course a few were reprints — but not all. And though Trapps Holmes may have had copy in hand it is unlikely that this would amount to more than a few weeks' supply.

When one considers that, at this time, Frank Richards was writing a full length Greyfriars and St Jim's story each week, serials for other papers, and at least an average of four stories a week for Trapps Holmes publications one can only acknowledge it all as a fantastic feat, and one which even the great Edgar Wallace in his prime would have been hard put to equal.

Curiously, Frank Richards seems to have had the impression that Trapps Holmes was a highly successful firm as his comments in the fifties show:

> "These comics were well circulated in their day, and were very well-paying propositions. They were utterly unlike the so-called 'comics' of the present day ... it was before the American trash invaded this country and vulgarised everything ..."

However, official records of the firm are still in existence and these show that it was not as successful as Frank Richards later supposed. Indeed, like the more famous Aldine Publishing House which lost over £250,000 between 1907 and 1932, they frequently found the going very hard indeed.

By 1919, George Holmes had disappeared from his home in Margate — when the Registrar of Stock Companies wanted to get in touch with him. Another director in the Midlands, who was eventually contacted, was obviously agitated that he was left to explain the firm's financial plight.

> "Trapps Holmes & Co. Ltd ceased to exist around March 1920, as the whole concern was insolvent. My firm lost over £1,000 as a creditor. The business consisted solely of the publishing of very cheap comic papers for children and very young people. After the last war the firm got deeper and deeper into debt, and it was compelled to cease business altogether through lack of funds..."

When these losses started is not exactly clear, but probably the increased price of paper during the First World War had its effect. But what Frank Richards did not realise was that his stories for *The Magnet* and *Gem* were so highly successful that they undoubtedly did a great deal to reduce the Trapps Holmes circulations.

How ironic that he who had built up his reputation with this firm and was its star author should be at least partly responsible for causing its downfall!

SAVE YOUR FLAGS.

LOUD LAUGHS AT LOW COST!

BREEZY BEN TICKLES EVERYBODY!

Chuckles

½d

RUMANIA

No. 56. Vol. 2.   PRICE ONE HALFPENNY.   January 30th, 1915.

THE COMICAL ADVENTURES OF BREEZY BEN AND DISMAL DUTCHY!

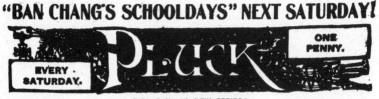

PLUCK

EVERY SATURDAY.

ONE PENNY.

[VOL. 5, No. 110, NEW SERIES.]

Our Long, Complete School Novel

The RIVALS

A TALE of ST. JIM'S.

A Splendid Story of Sport, Fun, and Adventure, and the Great Feud between the New House and the School House at St. Jim's College.

CHAPTER 1.
School House versus the New House.

JACK BLAKE came into Study No. 6 in the School House at St. Jim's, with a look of unusual excitement upon his face.

His two chums, Herries and Digby, were painfully busy with their preparation for the following morning, and they did not look up at his entrance.

"News, you chaps!" exclaimed Jack. "Shove that rot away. There's no time for that now!"

"Oh, bother your news!" said Herries crossly. "Run away and play! Go and eat coke! Buzz off and boil yourself! Can't you see I'm busy?"

"Look here——"

"Successit huic Nero," droned Herries. "Caligulae, avunculo suo——"

Jack picked up the book of Eutropius, and jerked him into a corner of the room.

"Now listen to me!" he exclaimed severely. "Talk about Nero fiddling while Rome was burning! Here are you two bounders swotting over rotten Latin when the honour of the School House is at stake!"

"Hallo, what's the row?" asked Herries, getting in-terested. "Those New House cads been up to their tricks again!"

"They soon will if we don't stop them," said Blake impressively. "The honour of the School House and the prosperity of St. Jim's generally is at stake, and here I find you with your nose in a beastly book. I wonder what would happen if I wasn't here to look after you kids!"

As Jack was the youngest of the three chums of Study No. 6, this was rather cool; but they let it pass.

"Well, get on," said Herries. "What's the game?"

"I've just come up from the hall. There's a notice on the board."

"Concerning us?" asked Herries and Digby together, wide-eyed.

"Yes, in a way. There's to be an election to-morrow for the new treasurer of the school clubs. You see how short the time is, and if we School House chaps are to prevent one of those New House bounders from getting in, we shall have to buck up."

And the three juniors looked at each other with a gravity becoming the seriousness of the situation.

A serious situation it was, from the point of view of Study No. 6, at all events.

Armitage, of the School House, had held the post referred

UNION JACK.—Vol. XII.—No. 294.

One Against Thirty!

A Story of Peril and Adventure Afloat and Ashore.

Specially told for "Union Jack" readers by CHARLES HAMILTON, Author of "Bold British Boys," "An Ocean Tragedy," &c., &c.

CHAPTER 1.

A Cry in the Night—The Search on the Sea—A Man with a Woman's Hair—At the Last Moment.

"Hark! Did you hear that?"

Eight bells had just struck on board the ship "Kangaroo," three days out from Melbourne. It was twelve o'clock, and a clear, starry night. To starboard the watch could see dimly the line of the Australian coast. To port the great Southern

caller for help. The keen-eyed lad scanned the sea in search of him. Fortunately the weather was calm, and the sea smooth, otherwise the quest would have been hopeless.

At a short distance from the ship Captain Desmond made the oarsmen a sign to cease rowing. The boat drifted. Then Desmond hailed the stranger.

"Ahoy, there! Where are you?"

"Help!"

Faintly came the reply, from right ahead of the boat. The oars played again; forward they went. Then the captain shouted again. No answer. Again and again. Still no response.

"Can't you see him, Jim?" cried the skipper, pale with anxiety. "Good heavens! is the poor fellow to drown within a few fathoms of our boat?"

"There's nothing here, sir," said his nephew doubtfully. "Ah—by George!"

He dropped the lantern and sprang into the sea. He had seen something that looked like floating seaweed, but the next moment he saw a pale, anguished face glimmering through it, and knew that it was human hair. Here, then, was the poor fellow who had at last given himself up for lost. Jim sprang instantly to save him.

The man was insensible, and Jim was glad of it, for it spared him the frantic struggles of a drowning man, always difficult to master. He took a firm grip upon the long, floating hair, and, with a jerk, brought up the pale face that ...ing beneath the surface.

"...messmates!" cried Jim lustily. ...nd the strong hand of

14

Supplement to The Gleam.

A MOST DRAMATIC LONG COMPLETE STORY.

February 6, 1902.

THE MAN WITHOUT A NAME.

WRITTEN BY CHARLES HAMILTON.

CHAPTER I.

Dick Leslie's Enemy.

Lights gleamed from the Arcade Saloon, reddening the unpaved plaza of the camp of Spotted Dog.

It was evening, and the miners had come in from the gulches; the Arcade was crowded.

At the bar, fists were thumping and glasses clinking, and raucous voices calling for tanglefoot.

At the further end of the rough shanty, dignified by the name of "saloon," was the faro layout.

There sat the banker, nickel silver box in hand, mechanically dealing the cards, with stolid face, but restless eyes.

Miners in dirty red shirts and crackers, Mexicans in gaudy serapes and braided calzoneros, lined the table, staking coin, gold-dust, or chips, as they pleased, and watching the turn of the cards with gamester's eagerness.

As a brawny digger, with a muttered curse upon his ill-luck, retired dead-broke, a young man took his place at the table. To him the banker nodded.

"Hello, Dick! Come to take a last look at the tiger? The boys tell me you are leaving Spotted Dog."

Dick Leslie returned the nod.

"That's the truth, Blinker. I have struck "ile." Nothing wonderful, you know; but enough for what I want to do. I leave camp by the stage in the morning."

Blinker was shuffling the cards for a new deal. When the play recommenced, Dick betted lightly. His only object was to while away the deadly dull evening of Spotted Dog, where there were no amusements but drinking, gambling, and shooting. Dick chose faro as the mildest of these gentle recreations.

A man, a stranger in Spotted Dog, had followed Dick Leslie when he entered the Arcade, and he remained ever near the young miner.

The stranger was a young man, only a year or two over thirty. His features were clear-cut, his complexion pale, his eyes large and piercing. He

"Do you mean to make a claim to that stake?" he asked.

"Decidedly!"

"It is mine, and you are perfectly aware of it!"

"On the contrary, it is mine, and you cannot fail to be aware of that!" responded the stranger, with an insulting smile.

"I appeal to the banker."

But the banker "really hadn't noticed, gents."

He was too wise to be drawn into the disputes of the gamesters. And the other players had been too intent upon their own game to take any heed of their neighbours'.

Clearly the dispute would have to be settled Spotted Dog fashion between the two claimants.

"You see," the calm, sneering tones went on, "you will find no one to back your impudent claim."

Dick Leslie's bronzed face grew dark with anger.

He saw that the stranger wished to pick a quarrel with him, though for what reason he could not in the least comprehend.

Dick was pacific by nature, but when he met a man spoiling for a fight he was by no means "backward in coming forward."

"I can see that you are looking for trouble," he remarked quietly. "Well, I am just exactly the kind of man you want to run against. If you claim that dust you are a liar and a thief!"

"Bully for you, Dicky," murmured the miners round. Their sympathy was all with their townsman and against the stranger.

The latter smiled cynically, and again laid his hand upon the dust—his left hand, while his right clutched the butt of his six-shooter.

Dick's strong hand shot out, gripped his collar, and spun him round, sending him to the floor with a crash before he could draw his weapon.

He rolled over, then sprang up, grinding his teeth, his features convulsed with fury.

Dick's hand went to his belt.

There seemed nothing for it now but a fight to a finish.

The stranger was springing forward, finger on trigger, murder in his flaming eyes.

But suddenly a ghastly change came over him. He stopped, his revolver clattered upon the

It secured his leg to a strong bolt set in the wall, giving him freedom over a space of a few yards only.

Not a prisoner of the Inquisition, not a hapless victim of the Council of Ten, was held more securely than this wretched captive in twentieth-century England.

The dungeon, deep in the foundations of a ruined abbey, was far from the sight of men. Its existence was known to but few, all of whom had the best reasons for keeping it secret.

There a prisoner might rave and yell with incessant iteration, and only the cold stone walls would fling back the echo of his cries.

"Save me! Will you not save me?"

So cried the dungeon's inmate in a despairing voice.

The man he addressed was a remarkable-looking individual. Nothing peculiar in form or features, but his expression was weird, strange, uncanny. He was dumb and he was deaf. Never the sound of human voice had broken upon the tomblike silence of his brain. Never a word passed his sealed lips. Ignorant, untaught, uncared-for, he knew not even the language of signs by which the mute may make his wishes known.

Between him and his fellow-men was a great gulf fixed. Of what he saw he could tell nothing. Of what he thought—if he thought at all—he could never speak. No man could ever learn what dwelt in the recesses of that darkened mind.

And yet, from the large eyes—soft and expressive as a gazelle's—beamed the ray of intelligence. And in his gaze was pity too, as he looked upon the prisoner. He saw that the man suffered, but not a word of the wild pleading could he comprehend.

He shook his head slowly. Of the signs equivalent to speech he knew the nod and the shake of the head.

The prisoner had thrown himself upon his knees before the mute, clasping his hands in frenzied beseeching.

Years of imprisonment in the dungeon had robbed the poor wretch of courage, of fortitude, of pride.

But at the mute's negative sign he rose, with a groan of hopeless misery.

"Fool that I am! He cannot hear! He does not know what I say. Yet he must know that I crave my liberty. Wretch, begone!"

The mute set down the food and drink he had brought to the prisoner.

The latter had raised his hand to strike, but he allowed it to fall again to his side.

The mute retired.

Alone, the prisoner paced the dungeon, his steps keeping doleful time to the clanking of his chain.

"Buried alive!" he muttered, "buried alive! Must this really be my tomb, as the villain threatened? Why did he not kill me outright? Some last scruple—some rag of con... stayed his hand. And he is my br... father's son, if not my mother's. He

...ng ...cer- ...did ?

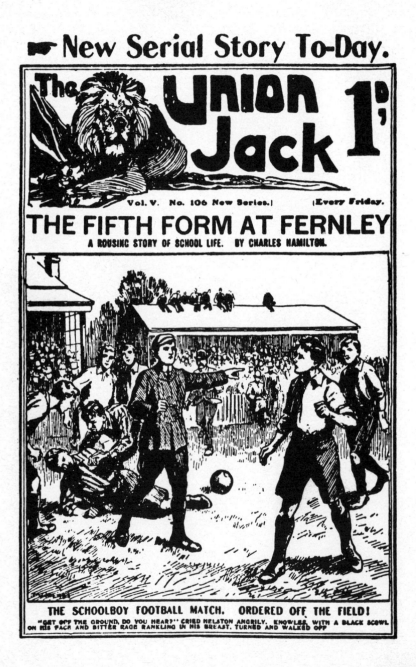

The UNION Jack 1ᴰ

Vol. V. No. 106 New Series.] [Every Friday.

THE FIFTH FORM AT FERNLEY

A ROUSING STORY OF SCHOOL LIFE. BY CHARLES HAMILTON.

THE SCHOOLBOY FOOTBALL MATCH. ORDERED OFF THE FIELD!

"GET OFF THE GROUND, DO YOU HEAR?" CRIED NELSTON ANGRILY. KNOWLES, WITH A BLACK SCOWL ON HIS FACE AND BITTER RAGE RANKLING IN HIS BREAST, TURNED AND WALKED OFF.

CHAPTER THREE

the Gem

Frank Richards started to make his mark in school fiction in 1906. For him this was an historic time. It was the year in which he wrote a story for *Pluck* entitled *Jack Blake of St. Jim's,* which was subsequently followed by other stories of the same school.

The Pluck stories dealt with the exploits of Jack Blake, a bright and bluff Yorkshire lad at St. Jim's. The school was divided into the School House, under Mr Kidd, and the New House under the sour and splenetic Mr Ratcliff, the denizens being known as Kids and Rats.

The junior Rats were headed by Figgins, Fatty Wynn — 'The Falstaff of the Fourth' — and a canny, sandy-headed Scot named Kerr.

Blake's aides were Herries, whom he had ousted from the junior captaincy, and Digby.

H.J. Garrish, the editor, suggested the inclusion of a 'swell' character, and so was born Arthur Augustus D'Arcy, 'the swell of St. Jims'. Garrish's editorial introduction hinted at a long run for the school.

But in another office of the Editorial Department of the Amalgamated Press juvenile publications there was strong competition at work. A new paper was about to be launched and this was to lead to not a little inter-office espionage. The scene was set, but not even stage manager Percy Griffith, the fiery-tempered wizard from Wales, and the prospective editor of *The Gem* was aware of it.

Frank Richards had worked for all the Harmsworth boys' papers and several of their comics, but he had not yet met the man to whom had been deputed the task of launching the new weekly. Time and fortune — with a little assistance — were to remedy that, and when they did meet the impact was to shake Frank Richards out of his customary reserve about personalities, so that he forever after dubbed Griffith 'the pushful Percy'.

Cecil H. Bullivant, also an editor at that time, and still alive today at 90, managed to compress a telling character study of Griffith into three words — "Clever — too clever!"

At the time that they met Frank Richards was living at Acton Vale, Middlesex, and used to travel all the way to Carmelite House by hansom cab. Approaching thirty, he was balding, wore pince-nez and looked extremely intellectual, rather like a university professor.

Calling at the famous building in 1907 for a routine discussion of future work with Henry J. Garrish, who was then editing *Pluck,* he followed his guide to what he imagined to be Garrish's office only to find himself ushered into the presence of Percy Griffith. Afterwards he remarked drily, "No doubt somebody pulled the strings." And no doubt he could have ventured a guess as to who did the string-pulling.

The Amalgamated Press was then riding on the crest of the wave with its boys' publications. Practically all of the older publishers in the field had been unable to withstand its onslaught on the juvenile market and both Brett and Hogarth House[1] had gone into liquidation a few months before this meeting. Carmelite House had not as yet experienced a failure. *The Boys Friend, Boys Realm, Boys Herald* trio for instance had been established by the firm's most successful man on the juvenile side, Robert Hamilton Edwards.

Managing editor of this group and a director of the firm, it

---

1 The Gem Library, in fact, was the title of a longstanding twopenny series issued by Hogarth House which was still on sale, but the owners of the copyright had other matters on their minds.

was no coincidence that an unusual amount of publicity and promotion had been lavished upon Edwards's brain child.

This support which had been amply rewarded even though there was nothing to distinguish any one of his magazines from the others except the masthead and the colour fixed to identify the paper. They shared the same direction, the same policy, the same artists and the same writers.

In 1907 Frank Richards had not yet become a school story specialist at Carmelite House for the very good reason that the Amalgamated Press as yet did not permit themselves such luxuries. He was not even the leading school story writer in Carmelite House. That distinction belonged to Henry St. John, with David Goodwin running a close second and soon to outstrip his rival.[2]

Percy Griffith would no doubt have been very glad to lure away either of these shining authors to add lustre to his new paper, but they mainly worked for *The Boys' Friend* group and Hamilton Edwards was too powerful and too autocratic for a fledgling editor to try any unwelcome poaching there.

However, his attention had also been seized by the St. Jim's series in *Pluck,* and H.J. Garrish, the editor of that paper, had not yet arrived at the eminence of a directorship and was easier game. In any case there was a much freer interchange of authors among the Libraries.

So Griffith went about angling Frank Richards into his own net. He need not have been too painstaking in his craftiness however, for Frank Richards could resist anything but temptation — when it was the lure of a new series. And so it was that he took what was to prove to be the most fortunate decision of his career to join Griffith on *The Gem.*

Griffith's idea was that he should invent a new school with suitable characters, and that the series — published under a new pen-name — should run on alternate weeks separated by stories by a variety of other authors. In the light of

2 When in 1905 the Amalgamated Press began to reprint their most popular serials in the small paper covered volumes of the *Boys' Friend Library* there were 31 school stories among the first 100 titles: 10 coming from St. John, 2 from Goodwin, and 4 from Frank Richards. Two of these were not reprints: *Tom Merry and Co* and *Tom Merry's Conquest* were new stories written specially to boost the Gem. The next 100 issues had 28 school stories with St. John and Goodwin reversing their 10-2 scores and Frank Richards dropping out completely.

subsequent events one may be forgiven for wondering if there was something ominous in this demand for a new pen-name.[3]

Such disguises were used freely, of course, the main trend being for a versatile author to use a different name for each category of his output. It looked to an impartial observer like a wanton dissipation of the goodwill attached to a well-known name, but our author had no qualms about that. Of the small army of sobriquet wielders who used Carmelite House he was the only one in whom the trick amounted to a monomania, and it was entirely appropriate that, during the last thirty years of his life, he should discard his real name of Charles Hamilton for everything except legal purposes and prefer to be known to all and sundry — including himself — by the most famous of his pen-names, Frank Richards.

Whilst Frank Richards was still elaborating the background for Tom Merry, Griffith got the paper under way. It is a pity that we do not know the editor's exact expectations. On the face of it, our author was only his second string. The honour of opening the run of *The Gem* went to Lewis Bird (Cecil Hayter) with *Scuttled.*[4] It was not until No.3 that a Richards' pseudonym was seen in the paper for the very first time, with *Tom Merry's Schooldays* by Martin Clifford, which continued in Nos. 5, 7 and 9.

Frank Richards' schoolboy characters made little use of front names. In common with the writer, they addressed each other and referred to each other, by surname. Tom Merry was the great exception. He was always either Tom, or, in full, Tom Merry, with even the masters adopting the same mode of address.

He begins as an orphan, eventually revealed as the son of General Merry of the Indian Army, and he has been reared by his old nurse, Miss Priscilla Fawcett, a lovable but fussy old lady dressed like Charley's Aunt.

She has been unable to grasp that her erstwhile baby is

---

[3] H.J. Drane of Trapps Holmes demanded a multitude of pseudonyms, giving the impression that he was either reluctant to build up an author or else was ashamed to admit that he published so much from one pen.

[4] He also wrote Nos. 4 and 10. Nos. 2, 6 and 8 were adventure stories by Nat Barr (Norman Goddard, who was killed in the First World War), Brian Kingston (Percy Longhurst) and Mark Glover (Clabon Glover), all names not used elsewhere.

now a sturdy youth of fifteen, and keeps him in velvet knickerbockered suits with lace collars, whilst his fair hair remains in long curls.

In spite of visual evidence to the contrary, she is convinced that her Little Lord Fauntleroy is delicate, and her morbid concern for his health finds expression in flannel vests, cod-liver oil, comforters, chest protectors, and continual dosage with *Terracotta Tablets for Tiny Tots* and other alliterative remedies — guying the once celebrated Dr William's Pink Pills for Pale People.

Tom is duly sent to Clavering School, where the young Headmaster is a Mr Victor Railton, an old Blue shown with a beard, which was certainly the artist's own idea since there is nothing at all about whiskers in the text. The only other member of the staff to survive coming changes was the heavily-Teutonic German master, Herr Otto Friedrich Schneider, inevitably the butt of the boys, with his battle-cry: "All poys require peating every morning."

Tom creates a sensation with his curls, velvet suit and long-winded, high faluting way of talking, but his two study mates, Henry Manners, the Captain of the Shell Form, and Monty Lowther, take him in hand and find him an apt pupil in boxing, cricket and slang.

The story is quite funny, though obviously a freak opening to the series. The only part of it which could be salvaged for future use was Miss Fawcett's fussing over Tom, which did sterling duty for the next thirty years.

The hero had to be normalised, a process carried out with such rapidity that by the third story, *Our Captain*, only Mr Railton's personal plea to Tom to stand down prevents him from being elected Captain of the School! By No. 9 he is the best batsman in all Clavering bar the Sixth, and scores a century. The stories were following a familiar light-hearted path, and if there was nothing sensational about them they were well above the average Amalgamated Press standard for the time.

The opportunities open to an author at the commencement of any such series are necessarily limited. The main character has to become cock-of-the-walk before attention can be given to assembling the cast of subsidiary characters who will give light and shade to the series, and some variety.

Martin Clifford was hustling Tom Merry into a position of leadership much faster than he was to do with Harry Wharton, Jimmy Silver or any of his other heroes, and had already begun the conflict with the Fifth Form which he planned to serve as a theme for a few weeks while he expanded the cast — a process, incidentally, which was not completed for eight years at Greyfriars.

He had already started to do this — when the upheaval occurred.

Although there was no reason for readers to be dissatisfied with the way things were developing, they did not get the chance to make their feelings known. Percy Griffith got in first. He was vaguely dissatisfied with the Clavering stories, though he couldn't quite put his finger on the cause. All he knew was that they were not up to his expected standard. And so he conceived the idea of moving Tom Merry from Clavering to St. Jim's and thus making the best of both series.

The Autobiography comments: 'This almost drove the author to resistance. He thought it a rotten idea, and disliked mixing up his works in this way . . . He fancied that Garrish might intervene and save him from being wholly devoured by the insatiable Percy. But his former editor made no sign and the pocket-dictator had his way, as he always did.'

In an early letter, Frank Richards added:

'I remember I did not like it a little bit when St. Jim's was transferred to the new paper, *The Gem*, and in fact I felt a little sore about it: however, I dare say it was all for the best. Things generally do turn out for the best, in the long run.'

Frank Richards always disliked editorial interference and would gladly have transformed Bernard Shaw's quip about teachers into: 'Those who can, write. Those who can't edit.' *He could have added: "Without good editors there would be fewer published writers."* But he shows here a curious blindness. Griffith's decision not only made *The Gem*, it also made Frank Richards.

He was not at that period capable of the sustained top quality output of his later days, nor capable of the finely defined characterisations which so distinguished his later stories. Whether he had remained incapable or not, he would never have had the opportunity of displaying such work in an ordinary serial. If *The Gem* had not been turned into a one-man paper, *The Magnet* could not have followed, and Frank Richards at his best would have been *primus inter pares* with Henry St. John, David Goodwin, John Nix Pentelow and the other school story serialists.

The essence of any story — and particularly any boys' story — is conflict: again, Frank Richards in 1907 was not capable of handling the subtler forms of that essential ingredient. Editor Griffith gave him, in brimming measure, a form that he could handle, and so sustained him through a difficult formative period.

Whatever misgivings the new Martin Clifford may have had, Griffith had none. He jettisoned his miscellaneous writers and pinned his faith to the new stories, thus showing both excellent judgment and considerable courage. No. 11 was titled *Tom Merry at St. Jim's*, and while the paper was to pass through some remarkable vicissitudes in its career of 1711 weeks, every subsequent issue dealt with just that — Tom Merry at St. Jim's.

Clavering was wound up on the pretext that a rich seam of coal had been discovered under the school and that the moneylender who held a mortgage on the property had promptly foreclosed. Mr Railton arranged with Dr Holmes of St. James' Collegiate School to accept such of his pupils as he wished to transfer and he and Herr Schneider took up posts under the Doctor. The boys dispersed to their homes ready for the change. Miss Fawcett, by giving Tom's school clothes away, and by 'turning on the waterworks' because she wanted to see her sweet Tommy once more as he used to be, got him once more into a velvet suit, and Tom thus attired entered St. Jim's as he had done at Clavering.

The joke did not improve by repetition, but as Blake and Figgins went to some trouble in trying to shunt the supposed freak from one House to another, it very neatly introduced the St. Jim's juniors and established the carefree atmosphere of friendly rivalry which pervades the St. Jim's tales.

As the leading lights in *Pluck* were Fourth Formers it had not been necessary to endow St. Jim's with a Shell. Tom Merry could hardly be demoted, which made it necessary to rectify the omission.

The Clavering Shell had looked upward, beating the Lower Fifth of whom only cursory mention was made and concentrating its rivalry on the Upper Fifth. The new arrangement made that impossible. The immigrants were locked in immediate conflict with the aborigines, forgot all their original ideas of being Upper School, and became more junior in outlook and antic. It was not until Tom Merry finally got rid of his velvet suit at the end of No. 11 that *The Gem* as we know it really began.

The change — whether Frank Richards realised or admitted it, or whether he still pined after the fulfilment of his original programme — was a godsend to him. At one swoop he enjoyed such an augmentation of his cast as could only happen once in a lifetime and which normally could only have been effected over many months or years by the gradual introduction of new characters in specially written stories which must, necessarily, have taken some of the emphasis off the regular performers.

He had already spent some time on the elaboration of the St. Jim's juniors and masters who were, in any case, more varied and attractive personalities than the Clavering squad. Manners and Lowther were mere bald sketches, still far removed from the quiet photographic-fiend and the inveterate joker they eventually became. Mr Railton was neither better nor worse than the Mr Kidd he was about to supplant, and Herr Schneider was simply the stock comic German master.

Only George Gore of the transferees was to play much further part in the stories, continuing his rôle of the moody bully. Against this, the lanky George Figgins, aided by the agreeable and athletic dumpling, Fatty Wynn, and the sagacious Kerr, who provided the brains of the Co. but was content to remain in the background, were in rivalry with the ebullient Blake, the stolid George Herries, the somewhat colourless Digby and 'the one and only', Arthur Augustus D'Arcy.

D'Arcy was to become as much the hallmark of *The Gem* as Billy Bunter was of *The Magnet* and there is a considerable case for regarding him as a more effective and certainly more convincing comedy figure.

The day was to come when Frank Richards would find his plots in the conflicts arising naturally out of the minutely detailed characters he had evolved over the years. Proof that he was at yet incapable of this came when *The Magnet* was launched on the strength of just forty-eight weeks' experience with *The Gem*. Greyfriars was without House division and to secure his conflict the author had to create a School for Aliens on the doorstep, and the rival public school, Highcliffe.

There was no need for that at St. Jim's.

With the 'Terrible Three' pitchforked into the middle of the existing internecine warfare, St. Jim's was in even greater turmoil than the turn-of-the-century Balkans. The School House fought with the New House juniors, and Blake and Merry were rivals for the leadership of the School House juniors. Blake and Figgins, as fellow Fourth Formers, sank their House differences and combined to keep the Shell from becoming too uppity, and everyone joined forces to resist aggression by the Fifth Form, Rylcombe Grammar School and bullying prefects. Meantime, Mr Ratcliffe kept interfering with the School House, producing some strange cross-currents of loyalty, and eventually even the Third Form was to stick its inky fingers in the pie[5].

Martin Clifford had served Frank Richards' apprenticeship

5   *The Gem* began as a halfpenny weekly and lasted in this form for 48 issues. The tales were lighthearted, inconsequential affairs, as indicated by such titles as *High Jinks at St. Jim's*, *Tom Merry's Washing Day*, *D'Arcy's Romance*, *The Diabolists* (dealing with the passing craze for diabolo and the only one of the early stories to suffer by its topicality: it was never reprinted), and *Figgins Fig Pudding* (flavoured with Syrup of Figs!). Ample proof of its intense popularity was then given by Griffiths' decision to expand The Gem into a penny paper and begin what he expected to be an imitation of it, The Magnet, at the old price of a halfpenny. Accordingly, on 15th February 1908, a new series of The Gem began from a fresh No. 1 and the first issue of The Magnet appeared with the same nominal dating. The first penny issue had a title of double significance: *The Gathering of the Clans*.

for him, and henceforward the rudimentary sketches which had had to serve for character drawing in the original concentration on Tom Merry's progress to Junior Captain were elaborated into finely-detailed portraits of boys of varying talent. He was now settled with a series which was to appear consecutively every week for the next thirty-two years of his life.

And so St. Jim's had been established with a maddeningly intricate but historic beginning. Frank Richards had created his establishment early, and major new characters were not required for some time. During Griffith's editorship, the newcomers were mainly 'lesser lights'[6].

One little known fact is that it was also in the pages of an early *Gem* that Frank Richards joined the ranks of the various artists who illustrated St. Jim's down the years. In No. 176, of 1911, he contributed an illustration of the famous D'Arcy for one of the inside pages.

For this he was paid the sum of seven shillings and sixpence but the talent there demonstrated suggests that he could well have become the regular illustrator as well as the author of the stories.

---

[6] Those who did join the school include Buck Finn (No. 51), Clifton Dane (No. 57), Harry Noble (No. 69), Lumley Lumley (No. 129) and then the exception — probably one of the finest characters of all time — Ernest Levision (No. 142) — though this boy, who was the subject of such fine character-building was no stranger, having been in the Greyfriars stories in *The Magnet*. Ethel Cleveland has been mentioned very early in the saga, in the ½d *Gem* No. 20, but being a female was merely one of the ancillary cast.

CHAPTER FOUR

the Magnet — and Billy Bunter

Once *The Gem* had evicted Tom Merry's Clavering co-tenants and settled down to an undisturbed run of St. Jim's stories, it never looked back.

By the time it was nine months old Percy Griffith arrived at the conclusion that the paper's popularity warranted promoting it from a halfpenny to a penny sheet, and that a companion at the old price could be relied on to pay its way.

Accordingly, the halfpenny series of *The Gem* was terminated at No. 48, and on 15 February 1908 the first number of the penny *Gem* was on sale alongside the first issue of the halfpenny *Magnet*.

Our author had earlier adopted the pen-name of Martin Clifford for *Gem* use — derived from Martin Rattler and Lytton's Paul Clifford — and to serve with *The Magnet* he now fixed on the name Frank Richards. 'Frank' came from Scott's *Frank Osbaldistone* and 'Richards' from his brother Dick's Christian name pluralised into a surname.

He was to reveal years later that he came to like this name so much that he almost adopted it legally, by deed poll.

In promoting *The Magnet* Percy Griffith was simply concerned to repeat his success with *The Gem*, and was no more worried about duplication than Hamilton Edwards had been with *The Boys Realm* and *The Boys Herald*[1] . But Frank Richards was far more curious and years later wrote:

> 'Griffith saw no reason why the new series should differ widely from *The Gem*. The author saw many reasons: and he made it quite different from the start. First came the new pen-name. This was an important matter to begin with. For names have a great effect, consciously, on an author, as they have consciously on everybody. Charles and Martin were one and the same person: but Charles did not write like Martin.'

The reader may doubt that a man will write differently when using different pen-names and feel that he is much more likely to be influenced by subject matter than pseudonyms. However, it cannot be disputed that, at the outset, Martin Clifford and Frank Richards did not resemble each other and, even now, when one compares the opening story in *The Magnet* with contemporary tales in *The Gem* it is difficult to accept that they come from the same man.

The opening of *The Gem* was a lighthearted throwaway having no bearing upon subsequent stories except that it established the essential gaiety of the series. In contrast, *Magnet* No. 1. *The Making of Harry Wharton* was painted in more sombre shades. It represented a considerable advance on any previous work by Frank Richards, and the finely-conceived character of the hero sounded the keynote of the series.

For the next thirty-three years the finest stories in *The Magnet* were those in which the darker side of Harry Wharton's complex nature came to the fore and his pride, temper and obstinacy involved him in conflict with authority and with his school-mates.

Wharton had only one feature in common with Tom Merry: he, too, was an orphan. He was the ward of his bachelor Uncle, Colonel James Wharton, who had been absent in India and on return said: "You have completely run wild under the charge of my sister, and I should not be doing

---

[1] The paper carried a series of our author's school stories about Cliveden, later republished in *The Dreadnought*.

my duty to my dead brother if I did not take you in hand and make at least an attempt to put you on a better road.

"You have grown up wilful and headstrong: you have grown into the habit of dictating to Miss Wharton and of overruling your tutor. Your education has been neglected . . ."

There was an unusually detailed description of the hero. 'He was a well-built lad, finely developed, strong and active. Handsome indeed was the face, with its well-marked features and large, dark eyes. But there was a cloud upon it, and in the dark eyes was a glint of suspicion and defiance. The whole manner of the boy was one of suppressed hostility, and the Colonel realised it keenly without words being spoken."

Colonel Wharton's remedy for his nephew's short-comings was to send him to his old alma mater, Greyfriars School, in Kent. In a bitter frame of mind, Wharton met Frank Nugent of the Greyfriars Remove on the train and they came to blows, Wharton fighting and acting like a wild cat, with snarling malice. But he was soon to redeem himself.

When some character in a Frank Richards' tale had to exhibit unsuspected nobility of character or heal a breach with either masters or school-friends, it was always a matter of interesting speculation to see whether he would do it by rescuing someone from drowning or by saving the same person from an attack by a tramp.

In fact, an editor of *The Magnet* some years later was heard to remark, "If all the Richards' characters fished out of an imminent watery grave were laid end to end they would dampen the entire length of the Great North Road!"

In this case, an early specimen of the genus 'road hog' tipped Nugent's hack over a bridge and Wharton staged a long and thrilling rescue. Nugent, brimming with gratitude once he had ceased to brim with water, took Wharton straightway under his wing, and all was calm and bright for a while.

Frank Richards had already used the name of Greyfriars anonymously in an earlier story, but save that a Mr Prout was a master at both there would seem to be no connection between the two schools. In *The Magnet* establishment, Mr

Quelch was already the master of the Remove, and Wharton was placed in Study No. 1 with Nugent, George Bulstrode the Remove Captain and bully, and Billy Bunter who was introduced thus: "The newcomer was a somewhat stout junior with a broad face and a large pair of spectacles." He was expecting a postal order, but the chief attribute, on which humorous situations hung, was his short-sightedness, which continually involved him in blunders.

The fat boy's part in the early stories could be said to be just one of the crowd. William George Bunter had been created many years previously, but had been put into cold storage. In a letter written in 1951, Frank Richards gave a more lucid explanation when he said:

'Bunter was first evolved as long ago as 1899. He was turned down by the publisher to whom he was offered, which discouraged the author and caused him to relegate the Owl to cold storage for years, and to give him a modest part when he did come to life at last in *The Magnet*. It is quite curious that best-sellers are generally turned down by publishers: a circumstance that ought to be very encouraging to young writers.'

Curiously there was quite a glut of Bunters floating around at that period. Frank Richards had himself given the name of Bill Bunter to a boozy and light-fingered tramp in the first Skimpole story in *The Gem* in 1907, and Sidney Drew, another well-known author, had also used the name for one of his boys in stories of Banthorpe School. But Drew's Bunter was slim and had none of W.G.B.'s traits.

Easily the most famous Bunter, however, was a Nervine Tonic, which had been advertised extensively since 1885. Bunter's Nervine claimed to cure almost everything from coughs and colds to toothache. A large bottle cost one shilling and a penny halfpenny. Perhaps the then young Frank Richards had needed a dose of this fantastical remedy to overcome some ailment whilst slaving over his earlier creations, and the name had stuck in his mind?

Dame Bunter, another of the tribe and one to whom the Fat Owl would undoubtedly have liked to have claimed relationship, was in charge of the Tuck Shop at Cliveden.

A fifth Bunter, also named Billy, had a most curious background. He was one of the boys of Blackminster School, an establishment featured in *The Vanguard*, a boys' paper published by the firm of Trapps Holmes — that produced so much of Frank Richards' work. As these tales, featuring Taffy Llewellyn and Co, predated *The Magnet* by some eight months they have caused quite a lot of discussion and conjecture over the years. But their author was certainly not Frank Richards.

H. Philpott Wright was the pen-name of the man who wrote them: actually J. Weedon Birch, an ex-officer rider to the Transport Chartered Companies of Rhodesia.

Little is known about him save that he later became a shareholder in the Aldine Publishing Company and a small-time publisher.

One accepts without question Frank Richards' statement that his Bunter was created — and rejected — some nine years earlier, for Frank Richards was always a truthful man. But the coincidence remains.

Frank Richards' reply to queries on the subject of the Bunter of Blackminster School was a terse one: he never read Trapps Holmes, nor any author's work except his own. And in any event one thing is certain. Philpott Wright's Bunter bore no resemblance to the Fat Owl, and his stories swiftly faded into oblivion.

When readers asked Frank Richards if there ever really was a Billy Bunter, his reply was:

> "Certainly there was, though the original Bunter was divided, like ancient Gaul, into three parts: derived from at least three different persons. His extensive circumference came from an editorial gentleman who, to Frank's eye at least, seemed to overflow the editorial chair and almost the editorial office. His big spectacles were borrowed from a relative of Frank's, who had been wont to peer at him somewhat like an Owl in boyhood days. His celebrated postal order, which he was always expecting but which seldom came, was a reincar-

nation of a cheque which a certain person constantly expected but which did not often material-
ise, and on the strength of which that person was
generally anxious to borrow a pound or two."

At the time of writing his Autobiography during the
Second World War, and with people he would mention in the
book still alive, he was loath to hurt their feelings. As they
have all now long departed this life a further elucidation is in
order.

The fat editor was undoubtedly Lewis Ross Higgins, editor
of the comic paper *Chuckles* 1914 to 1919, and on the staff
of many comic papers prior to this. A Welshman like Percy
Griffith, he was an enormous man, almost the prototype of
G.K. Chesterton for whom he was often mistaken. Unfortunately his size was attributable to a glandular disease and he
did not live long. A very clever cartoonist and an art critic for
Punch he was the artist 'Frank Nugent' in *The Greyfriars
Herald* as well as illustrator of the Herlock Sholmes parodies
by-lined 'Peter Todd', but written by Frank Richards, in yet
another guise.

It was also in Lewis Higgins' paper that a short series of
Greyfriars stories appeared with Dick Trumper & Co of
Courtfield County School. A few of these were written by
Frank Richards but the majority were by other writers.

Higgins, with the fruity laugh, a cigarette always dangling
from his lips, was a kindly, genial man with a great sense of
humour. He died at only thirty-four at his home in St.
Albans, in 1919.

Bunter's spectacles came from Frank Richards' young
sister Una, who had unfortunately suffered bad sight since
early childhood. The celebrated postal order was based upon
the optimism of his older brother, Alex, also attempting to
break into journalism. Like Billy Bunter he was always
expecting something to turn up in the post — but it was
invariably a rejection slip.

The surname of Bunter is not so unusual as many people
imagine. Families of that name have been traced in the West
Country as far back as the eighteenth century.

Readers who first became acquainted with Greyfriars during

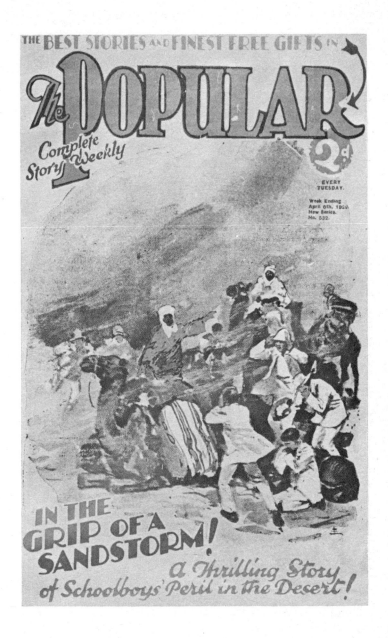

THE BEST STORIES AND FINEST FREE GIFTS IN

The POPULAR

Complete Story Weekly

2d

EVERY TUESDAY.

Week Ending
April 6th, 1929.
New Series.
No. 532.

IN THE GRIP OF A SANDSTORM!

A Thrilling Story of Schoolboys' Peril in the Desert!

New Size! New Stories! Great Free Gift Number!

SCHOOL AND SPORT 1½d

No. 25. Vol. II.   Week Ending June 3rd, 1922.   EDITED BY H. A. HINTON.   PRICE 1½d.

P. G. H. FENDER (SURREY).
No. 1 County Captains Series.

LONDON & NORTH WESTERN RY. ENGINE
No. 1 British Railway Engines Series.

THE ORANG-OUTANG
No. 1 Wild Animal Series.

SCOTS GUARDS
No. 1 British Regiments Series.

Four Free Photo Plates inside

The GEM 1½d

No. 582. Vol. XIII. April 5th, 1919.

THE STONY STUDY!

TOM MERRY DELIVERS THE GOODS!

(A Screamingly Funny Scene in the Splendid Long Complete School Tale in this Issue). 5-4-19

The BOYS' FRIEND 1d.

OUR MOTTO IS: "PLAY THE GAME!"

No. 823, Vol. XVI. New Series.]　　　ONE PENNY.　　　[Week Ending March 17th, 1917.

THE STRUGGLE IN THE WOODS! JIMMY SILVER & CO. TO THE RESCUE!

LOVELL'S LUCK!

A Magnificent New Long Complete Story, dealing with the Adventures of Jimmy Silver & Co. at Rookwood School.

By OWEN CONQUEST.

The 1st Chapter.
The Intruder.

"I'm not going to stand it!"
Thus said Jimmy Silver as he entered the end study. The usual cheerful expression on Jimmy's face had vanished, to be replaced by one of annoyance and indignation.

There was no reply to Jimmy's exclamation. Lovell and Raby and Newcome were grinding out lines, all they were worth, and they were utterly ignorant of Jimmy Silver's presence.

"I won't stand it!" said Jimmy emphatically. "Seventy-five lines!"

Still there was no reply. Jimmy Silver approached the table and sat down on a vacant chair.

"I'm simply not going to stand it!" he exclaimed, with a wrathful wot-you "Crisis!"

Lovell and Jimmy Silver's fag on the table at which Lovell and his chums were hard at work. Jimmy Silver intended to emphasise the meaning of his remark, in some way, and he succeeded without the shadow of doubt.

Paper and pens flew off the table as though caught by a terrific gust of wind. Ink, too, was spilled in great quantities.

Lovell and Raby and Newcome jumped up in great alarm.

"Fathead!" exclaimed Lovell, in tones of annoyance. "What did you do that for?"

"I'm not going to stand it!" cried Jimmy Silver.

"Well, sit down then!" retorted Lovell sharply.

"Don't be a silly chump, Lovell! I said I'm not going to stand it."

"I know you did," replied Lovell. "And there's no reason why you should. There's an arm-chair over there in the corner. I know it's a bit gammy, but it'll hold you all right."

During this roasted

"Seems to me you're getting denser and denser, Lovell," he said, never said a word about sitting down. Look here, I'm not going to——"

"There he goes again!" interrupted Lovell, with a shake of the head. "Why don't you squat down, Jimmy, and let us get on with our lines? You've marked up about half of them with your cleanness?"

"Blow your lines!" snapped Jimmy Silver. "Lines don't count at a time like the present!"

"Why not?"

"Because the future of the end study is at stake."

"Oh, come off it, do, Jimmy!" said Lovell. "Why don't you roll

(Continued on the next page.)

what you've got to say, and have done with it?"

"It's all Bootles' fault!"

"What is?"

"Why, the planking of the new kid on to us!" explained Jimmy Silver.

"What!" gasped Lovell. "A new kid coming into this study?"

"That's the long and short of it," said Jimmy Silver.

"Can't be did!"

"That's what I told Bootles," said Jimmy Silver. "But he wouldn't listen to reason. It appears that the Head's wish we look after the new kid, because he's delicate—a regular old crock, you know."

"What's the Head think we are, a lot of nurses?"

"Peace, I call it!" growled Raby.

"I'm not going to stand it!" said Newcome determinedly.

"That's what I said!" exclaimed Jimmy Silver. "But I fail to see what we can do in the matter. You can't buck against the Head."

"Suppose not," said Lovell. "But I bet the new kid will be so pleased with the welcome he receives that he'll be only too eager to shift into another study within a week."

"Of course, there's no reason why we should make him too comfortable."

"No fear!"

"Tap!"

"Here is the bounder, I bet!" said Jimmy Silver, as there was a faint tap on the door.

"Come in!"

The door opened slowly, but no figure appeared.

"Come in, fathead!" roared Jimmy Silver. "It's cold with the door open!"

The Fistical Four walked for the visitor to enter. Suddenly a face appeared round the side of the door, and gradually the full form of the newcomer appeared.

Jimmy Silver & Co. gasped.

The new boy was a very queer object. He was dressed in an overcoat that reached to his ankles, his hands were clothed in thick woollen gloves, and an enormous muffler adorned his neck. On his nose was a pair of rather large spectacles, and in his hand he held a big bag. As Jimmy Silver observed afterwards, he was a sight for the gods.

"I hope you don't mind my intruding," said the new-comer, "but I have been informed by Mr. Bootles that I am to share this study. My name is Bishop, and I'm quite new to Rookwood."

The new boy finished up his remarks with a sniff.

"Got a cold?" asked Jimmy Silver.

"Yes, unfortunately," said Bishop, drawing an enormous handkerchief from a capacious pocket. "I seem never to be without colds and coughs."

"Tincture of quinine is supposed to be very good for a cold," ventured Jimmy Silver.

"Yes, I know," said Bishop, with a smile. "I have plenty in my bag."

"Have you really?"

"Yes," said Bishop. "By the way, would you mind if I disrobed, and at the same time emptied my bag?"

"Not a bit!"

"Thank you so much!"

Bishop put his bag up on the table, and took off his coat and muffler.

The Fistical Four eyed him wonderingly.

"I wonder whether you would mind my putting my medicine bottles on the mantelshelf?" asked Bishop politely.

"Oh, any old thing!" replied Jimmy Silver rather irritably.

The new boy opened his bag, and, withdrawing a bottle, placed it very fully on the mantelshelf. Then he took out another bottle, and placed it beside the first.

the latter part of its run might be excused if they thought that the status quo of the Remove Form had been maintained unchanged right from the beginning. It actually took Frank Richards 559 weeks to gather together 38 of the 39 characters listed in *Magnet* 1659.

In that period a total of at least eighty different Removites had appeared on the scene. Many of course had left the school, a few had been expelled, others, like old soldiers, had simply faded away. A fair number, of course, were not invented by the 'genuine' Frank Richards, for other authors wrote some 'substitute stories' under this pen-name from time to time. But these characters had very short careers.

Already at the school when *The Magnet* began its run were Frank Nugent, George Bulstrode, Peter Hazeldene, Harold Skinner, Dick Russell and Billy Bunter, and all these juniors were still there at the last issue.

Bob Cherry, with his cheery "Hallo, Hallo, Hallo", made his arrival in No. 2 and so there were then three members of the future Famous Five. Marjorie Hazeldene was introduced in No. 5, and this pretty girl of Cliff House School was to feature quite a lot in future stories as well as to cause deep upset for Frank Richards as the reader will learn later.

The author was quick to bring out Bob Cherry's devotion to Peter Hazeldene's sister — and one must call it devotion, as love was strictly taboo in the Greyfriars saga.

Hurree Singh, who first came to Greyfriars in No. 6, had a much earlier origin than *The Magnet*. He was in the Third Form at Netherby School almost a year previously, in *The Marvel*. His introduction is quite amusing.

> "My boys, this is your new form-fellow, Hurree Singh," said Mr Lumsden, with a wave of the hand . . . The Indian boy was left alone with his new form-fellows. He was surrounded at once by eager seekers after knowledge. "I say, Inky, where do you come from?" asked Knowle. The Hindoo lad looked puzzled. "My name is not Inky," he said in excellent English. "My name is Hurree Jamset Ram Singh."

The story of Hurree Singh's eventual enrolment in the

Remove is quite extraordinary. In time he left Netherby School for Beechwood Academy, run by Herr Rosenbaum, which was opened in Kent. En route, as it were, circumstances compelled him to stay for a short time at Greyfriars School and, naturally enough, he did not want to leave, so he hid in the box-room. Another boy might have been beaten, but as a result of this stratagem Hurree Singh was allowed to stay at Greyfriars for the rest of the run of the paper. But one wonders if he learned much. Certainly, as he had spoken excellent English before entering Greyfriars one cannot allow any marks to the English lessons imparted by Mr Quelch.

Curiously, the last remaining member of the Famous Five to arrive did so in *Magnet* 151, right on the heels of Fisher T. Fish. Johnny Bull was blunt, honest and rather outspoken, and the least well-liked of the group.

Despite the charm of Greyfriars it is generally accepted that the first few years' output contained quite a few pot-boilers. The stories certainly seem to be cluttered up with unnecessary characters and, by and large, *The Gem* yarns were far superior. Even so, the foundations were being laid for some really first class characterisations, and series, in the years to come.

Herbert Tudor Vernon Smith, The Bounder, arrived in No. 119 bemused and in a drunken state, and it was only because Dr. Henry Locke, the Headmaster, owed his father money that he was allowed to stay.

Horace James Coker, the 'duffer' of the Fifth, had seemingly been at the school from the very beginning, though he was not mentioned until *Magnet* 143. The early Coker was much different from the later version. This time he was in the Shell, but his Aunt Judy, complete with umbrella, persuaded Dr. Locke to move this 'much older boy' up to The Fifth. The logic, perhaps, was that he might just as well be a fool in The Fifth as in a lower form.

Coker, incidentally, was based on Frank Richards' brother Dick, a much more sturdy member of the family and one who fancied himself as a leader.

Readers with a flair for detection may have suspected that Martin Clifford and Frank Richards were one and the same when D'Arcy visited Greyfriars, and from time to time the Greyfriars juniors were mentioned as being with the St. Jim's characters. More astute readers still would have been alerted by the fact that the St. Jim's tales in *Pluck* were written by Charles Hamilton and those in *The Gem* by Martin Clifford. But any reader voicing his suspicion would soon be put in his place by an editorial statement recording the three authors meeting, and this pretence was carried on right through the history of *The Magnet* and *The Gem*.[2]

Thus Percy Griffith had successfully launched two juvenile papers, but he was not destined to stay at the helm much longer, nor to see *The Magnet* and *Gem* become the best loved periodicals of all time.

[2] For full list of Frank Richards' pseudonyms, see Appendix 2.

CHAPTER FIVE

the years of change

Just as soon as Frank Richards had established a steady market for his stories he indulged a desire that had been with him since boyhood. He started to travel. And he visited many countries prior to the First World War.

His manuscripts would arrive at the editorial offices in long envelopes bearing many strange postmarks, and always beautifully typed. They hardly, if ever, required any editorial revision except when, as occasionally happened, Frank Richards' copy was too long to fit the available space and had to be cut to length.

The stories used to reach the Companion Papers, as the *Magnet* and *Gem* were called, from the Austrian Tyrol, the Bay of Naples and the French Riviera, and there were occasions when the margins of one of the pages of a *Gem* or *Magnet* manuscript would be covered with numbers, some recurring at frequent intervals. There is reason for supposing that these figures represented the permutations of an 'infallible' system designed by the author to break the Bank at Monte Carlo!

All Frank Richards' manuscripts were typed with a purple ribbon. In those days all typewriter ribbons were this colour. They were impregnated with copying ink, so that duplicates might be made on the tissue-leaved copying books of the

period employing a screw-press of the kind one still encoun-
ters in sale rooms. Frank Richards continued to use ribbons
of this kind and colour on his typewriter long after their
original purpose had been superseded. He used them, in fact,
for the whole of his life.

Many of his correspondents have commented on this and
some have concluded that this colour ribbon suited his failing
eyesight better than stark black. This might just be true,
though recent experiments in America lead one to doubt it.
His conservative nature is probably the chief reason why he
did not change.

With the sudden and mysterious departure of Percy
Griffith from the A.P. in 1911, it was Herbert A. Hinton who
was next to receive those purple-inked manuscripts, and
Frank Richards found him much more easy to get on with
than the 'pushful Percy'.

At the same time, C.M. Down was promoted to Chief
Sub-editor, whilst other members of the staff included G.R.
Samways, Noel Wood-Smith, H.W. Twyman (who later edited
the Union Jack), Stanton-Hope, Hedley O'Mant, W.E. Pike
and R.T. Eves.

Kaiser Wilhelm soon broke up this happy band, however,
and H.A. Hinton found himself in wartime with a skeleton
staff and even more papers under his control — including the
green-covered *Boys Friend*.

Hinton wanted to put the circulation up — with the aid of
Frank Richards, of course. A brand new school was to be
introduced, different from St. Jim's, and a little different
from Greyfriars. He also suggested that the leader of the
usual trio of boys should be named Jack Fisher.

What Frank Richards thought about this proposal is not
known. From his earliest days he had always shown an
exceptional facility for memorably naming his characters. He
completely avoided the alliterative names which so delighted
the Victorians, names such as Ned Nimble and Ted Torment.
Instead, he unerringly found names whose very sound
suggested the kind of character he wished to convey.

What better bullies or cads could we have than Crooke,
Gore, Skinner and Snoop, for example? And what better

happy heroes than Tom Merry or Bob Cherry?

Mr Paul Prout could not sound more portly or pompous. Every character Frank Richards created was titled appropriately, for he had a great liking for onomatopoeia.

So Rookwood School and Jimmy Silver came into existence, and probably this boy was the most sensible and best balanced lad in all school fiction. His affectionate nickname 'Uncle James' is an indication of this. It is not without significance that he is the only one of the trio including Wharton and Merry to have such an affectionate handle to his name.

There was an easy-going, philosophical streak to Jimmy Silver, placid, patient, tolerant, always giving sensible advice, extremely good-tempered and invariably with a cheerful grin on his face; he was an ideal boy to have as a chum.

The Rookwood stories, which featured a Classical and a Modern side, were almost certainly based on Frank Richards' old school at Thorn House. Being only virtually a third of the length of a *Magnet* or *Gem* story they were much quicker and easier to write, and it was quite common for six stories to arrive in the editorial office at once.

The pen-name used for these stories was Owen Conquest, and was probably editorially suggested — evidence the fact that the author always avoided giving an explanation for this choice of name, and in fact never did.

Rookwood had been mentioned in an earlier Greyfriars story, when Bob Cherry had biked over to Hampshire and had seen the Rookwood football team in action.

Jimmy Silver made his entrance on to a smaller stage than the other main schools. Boys already at Rookwood included the three Tommies: Tommy Dodd, leader of the Modern juniors, curly-haired and with a prominent nose, and his two trusty friends Tommy Cook and Tommy Doyle. Others were 'The Fistical Three' — Arthur Edward Lovell, George Raby and Arthur Newcombe — and masters included the Head, Dr Chisholm D.D., M.A., and Mr Bootles, Master of the Classical Fourth, later to be replaced by Richard Dalton an ex-professional boxer — not without some initial worries and problems.

Mr Bootles inherited a million pounds and was more fortunate than the Greyfriars and St. Jim's masters who were never able to retire from their teaching.

Herbert A. Hinton eventually was called to the colours, but not before suffering the fright of his life when his star author made an unsuccessful attempt to do his duty and fight for his country. Frank Richards related the story of his attempt to join the army quite amusingly in his Auto-biography, and one must admire his patriotism at the age of forty-one. He was rejected on the grounds of poor eyesight and a general low standard of fitness after being examined at Mill Hill Barracks. He was proud of the medical certificate which gave the reasons for his rejection. At least he had tried. And he was wont to show the certificate to friends and acquaintances in later years.

With Herbert Hinton now in the Coldstream Guards, where he held the rank of Captain, forty-four year old John Nix Pentelow became the third editor of *The Magnet* and *The Gem* and the most controversial.

Frank Richards had had his troubles with Percy Griffith and slight upsets with Hinton from time to time but these were insignificant compared with his furious clashes with Pentelow, and the anger that the editor roused in him remained for the rest of his life.

Pentelow was tall and broadly built, a clean-shaven man with crisp white hair. He spoke very softly and regarded the world through mild, grey-brown eyes in a manner that was rather disarming. He was born at Huntington, the son of a grocer, and was a schoolmaster and an officer in the Customs and Excise before coming to London to take up editorial work.

An expert on cricket, he had written many textbooks on the subject and was also a first-class school story writer. Unfortunately he had suffered severe financial loss when involved in a cricket publication with A.C. McLaren, the famous Test batsman, and the worry of this was said to have prematurely aged him.

He was also very deaf, but scorned wearing a hearing aid. He had the habit of suddenly breaking off a conversation and yarning about some cricket match and his visitors found this most frustrating. Conversation with him had to be carried on, of course, at the top of one's voice and could be heard down all the corridors of Fleetway House. Even after they'd left him, many people still found themselves shouting. In these circumstances, Pentelow's first meeting with the mild-voice Frank Richards was not a success.

Before becoming editor, Pentelow had been judge of a Greyfriars story competition in the office next door and was regarded as someone with a considerable knowledge of Greyfriars and St. Jim's as he had read all the back issues. It should be mentioned here, but dealt with more fully later, that substitute stories had been inserted in *The Magnet* and *The Gem* when genuine stories were not available, and that as an outcome of his interview with Pentelow, Frank Richards was left with the impression that the editor was quite prepared to write all the stories in both papers himself if copy did not come in on schedule.

Gentleman though he was, Frank Richards' answer to this was well-nigh unprintable, and the outcome was that he slammed out of the office and stormed off in very high dudgeon.

Later, swallowing his pride, and knowing that Pentelow was only a wartime stop-gap, Frank Richards did write more stories for *The Magnet* and *Gem*, but these contributions were few and far between. It was during this period, in fact, that he concentrated upon his Rookwood tales.

Unfortunately all the reports we have of this feud between editor and author are necessarily one-sided. One has only heard the views of the writer. There is certainly no evidence that Pentelow excluded Frank Richards' stories to make room for his own. The stock books for the period give this the lie. Pentelow used his own work only because the cupboard was bare, Frank Richards declining to contribute on anything like his former scale.

When he did contribute, he co-operated — evidence the fact that he used characters that were not his own in some of his stories, most memorably Piet Delarey, the South African junior, and Phyllis Howell. But the truth must be that, overall, Frank Richards and John Nix Pentelow simply never got on.

Easily the greatest controversy during Pentelow's reign was caused by *Magnet* No. 520 (1918) *A Very Gallant Gentleman*, written by Pentelow himself, and in which he killed off Courtney of the Sixth in a fire. At first sight this seemed an act of crass stupidity. Recent years have brought more facts on the matter to light, however, and it transpires that readers were confusing the Greyfriars Courtney with Frank Courtenay of Highcliffe. So, after obtaining guidance from higher authority, Pentelow killed the former lad off.

Why Frank Richards, who had created Courtney in the first place, was not consulted in the matter it is difficult to say — though, to be fair, the character was only a minor one. Frank Richards, however, decided that he should have been consulted and was indignant. It was one more black mark against Pentelow.

On the other hand during the war years the editor performed a great service to all those readers who were thirsting for more intimate knowledge of their schoolboy heroes. To satisfy their craving he introduced *The Greyfriars Gallery* and *The St. Jim's Gallery* in *The Magnet* and *Gem* respectively. The former ran for 102 weeks and the latter ended only when Pentelow relinquished his editorship.

Regular readers of Frank Richards' stories found his characters very real. The reader who stayed with a paper for a few months, in fact, probably knew more about the personalities of the leading juniors than he did of those of most of his schoolfellows. Yet Richards was remarkably restrained in his direct description, and there was no overloading of detail. He was artistically justified in this respect, but many readers regarded his method as unnecessarily spartan and there was a continuing demand for more information about the series characters.

In Pentelow's *Galleries* on the other hand were detailed pen-pictures of the characters in both schools with a mass of information from earlier stories — all garnished with portraits.

In time, these supplements had more information on file

than Scotland Yard. There were even detailed lists of the heights and weights of the boys and their ranking as boxers or athletes.

Much of this information was, of course, dredged up from the imaginations of the sub-editors working in what Frank Richards called "the menagerie". It was certainly not to be found in the stories. And the satisfaction of this boyish need to know more about a hero was not untouched with a certain cynicism. There was an instance when a 'portrait' of Harry Manners of St. Jim's reappeared a few years later as an equally authentic 'likeness' of Harry Wharton of Greyfriars.

This was giving the public what it wanted, whilst demonstrating the gulf that lay between the methods of the editor and author. Bob Cherry played a leading role in the stories for over fifty years. The regular reader might not know what he himself would do in certain circumstances, but he would know quite well how Bob would react.

When he knew the characters so intimately it is thought provoking to discover that the complete sum of what he learned from Frank Richards about Bob Cherry's appearance was that he was sturdy, had a mop of fair hair and — unless his comrades maligned him — biggish feet.

It was during war-time that Frank Richards was called on yet again to launch a new series of stories. Once again these were for *Boys Friend Weekly*, and they were set in the backwoods of Canada, in British Columbia. Here was quite an interesting idea of recording the imaginary schoolboy adventures of Frank Richards at Cedar Creek, as told by his old friend Martin Clifford.

A host of characters was introduced: Frank Richards, the boy, Bob Lawless and Vere Beauclere, his own special friends, and the fat boy Chunky Todgers. Also Ethel Meadows, the Headmistress, Dicky Bird & Co, and Cedar Creek's rivals at Hillcrest School. Western outlaws were introduced into the stories, and not a little villainy caused the added attraction of the arrival of Sergeant Laselle of the North West Mounted Police.

Frank Richards also pulled no punches when he wrote one yarn concerning a substitute story being published in a spot in the local paper usually reserved for 'Frank Richards, the boy author'.

Frank Richards clearly derived a great deal of satisfaction from writing these stories of his imaginary schooldays — even to the extent of almost living out some of his childhood fantasies. And with the *Penny Popular* at this time reprinting his earlier stories there was no question but that he was rapidly becoming the greatest asset the Amalgamated Press ever had.

Frank Richards was far from being a vindictive man, and quite speedily forgave people whom he believed to have wronged him. Pentelow was the exception — for an accumulation of all of the reasons that have already been stated, and perhaps for another. Pentelow scorned to model himself upon Frank Richards when writing Greyfriars and St. Jim's stories. He wrote in his own natural style. And this was almost the perfect antithesis of the creator's sparkle. It was sentimental — or even Victorian — in tone and lacked verve and punch.

To do this to *his* series might have been the unforgiveable sin in Frank Richards' eyes. Certainly he never did forgive John Nix Pentelow.

The end of the First World War saw C.M. Down back home before Hinton, and he resumed the editorship. Pentelow went on to several other papers before retiring from *The Boys Realm* in 1924.

In spite of his stormy relationship with Frank Richards, it should be stated that Pentelow was highly thought of at Fleetway House. He was regarded as being somewhat akin to Doctor Locke, the Headmaster of Greyfriars, a firm and fatherly figure, kind and a perfect gentleman.

He was presented with a handsome silver cigarette box by all his colleagues, when he retired to Carshalton, Surrey, where he died in 1931, aged only 59 years.

CHAPTER SIX

the Bessie Bunter affair

Reginald T. Eves could be said to have been a slightly worried man in early 1918. This was not connected with the papers he had been editing as a wartime deputy. The circulation of *The Penny Popular, Boys Friend Weekly* and *Boys Friend Library* were all healthy.

The chief cause of his concern was that when the war finally ended, and editors called to the colours returned to their old positions, he would either be demoted or — worse still — lose his job altogether.

There was only one solution, and that was to start up a brand new paper of his own.

At that time he was sharing an office with John Nix Pentelow, wartime editor of *The Magnet* and *Gem* and the daily flood of letters received from *Magnet* girl readers indicated that there was a latent demand for a school story paper for girls. If girls enjoyed reading about the boys of Greyfriars surely they would enjoy reading about the girls of Cliff House? They had never before had the chance to prove whether they would or they wouldn't — and so the basic idea of the *School Friend* was born.

The Cliff House school and its girls — chiefly Marjorie Hazeldene and Clara Trevlyn — had appeared in many of the early *Magnet* stories, and now an additional bright idea was also suggested: why not have a sister for Billy Bunter and call her Bessie?

At this stage in the war it was not possible to start new papers, owing to the rationing of newsprint. But, wasting no time, Reg Eves made a special trip to see Frank Richards, then living at Hampstead Garden Suburb, and put the suggestion to him.

Reg Eves remarked afterwards that he almost failed to recognise Richards at first, as he had grown a beard. Whether this was to save steel for the war-effort is not known, but it had been shaved off by the next time he visited Fleetway House.

Frank Richards was full of enthusiasm for the new venture. To get into his stride it was suggested that he write a 60,000 word story for the *Boys Friend Library* entitled *Bessie Bunter of Cliff House School*. It was in this same series that he had enjoyed tremendous success some years previously with two tales of Highcliffe: *The Boy Without a Name* and its sequel *Rivals and Chums*. No doubt Bessie Bunter would be a big success, too.

While this was awaiting publication, however, it was inevitable that Frank Richards — groping around for an idea, and already having written many stories featuring the Cliff House girls — should decide to write a Greyfriars story about his new character Bessie. So Bessie Bunter first appeared in *Magnet* No. 582, dated 5 April 1919, some six weeks before the *School Friend* commenced!

The front cover showed Billy's fat sister for the first time, sitting in a Courtfield bun-shop. Her hair is in long tresses, she is carrying a rolled umbrella and there is a pleasant look on her rather plump 'identical to Billy' face. The artist was C.H. Chapman — and so he must claim to have been the original illustrator.

Christened Elizabeth Gertrude Bunter, Bessie was the daughter of Mr Samuel Bunter, a stockbroker, who worked amongst the 'bulls and bears' of the City. Her home was Bunter Villa in Reigate, Surrey, and their family car was a single Ford, though like her brothers Billy and Sammy, she strongly fancied that she lived at Bunter Court with liveried servants and five or six Rolls Royces.

Such was the brilliant characterisation of Frank Richards' writings that although Bessie was almost a carbon copy of Billy she existed, somehow, as a separate character and certainly possessed a more domineering nature.

There was no love lost between the younger members of the Bunter family. Frank Richards showed this in a delightfully-written passage from one of his earlier stories. Billy owes Bessie five shillings:

> 'Five shillings was not a large sum, but if it had been five hundred thousand pounds Bessie Bunter could scarcely have dwelt on the subject with more eloquence. In season and out of season, Elizabeth Bunter dwelt on that topic tirelessly. Bessie was, in Billy's opinion, a cat. Bessie's opinion of Billy could not be expressed so laconically. Her vocabulary in the subject was very extensive indeed. Only on one subject could Billy and Bessie agree. That was the subject of Sammy. They heartily agreed that Sammy was a little beast.'

Later, when Billy was leaving home, Bessie came running after him.

> 'Bunter smiled, at the moment of parting Elizabeth Bunter seemed to realise what a nice brother he was, and wanted to say goodbye. Perhaps to hand him a packet of toffee for the train. Bunter's fat face was quite genial as Bessie rolled up.
>
> "You're going away?" gasped Bessie.
>
> "Yes."
>
> "Not coming back?"
>
> "N-n-no!"
>
> "Well, then, that five shillings —"
>
> "Wh-a-at?"
>
> "That five shillings," gasped Bessie Bunter.
>
> William George Bunter stared at her. His geniality vanished. It was not to say an affectionate farewell that Bessie hastened after him — it was not to give him a packet of toffee to eat in the train. It was to raise, once more, the old distasteful

question of five shillings.'

Eventually the first number of the *School Friend* appeared on 17 May 1919 and the opening story related how Bessie Bunter arrived at the school. The story was entitled *The Girls at Cliff House*. Bessie had a pet, complete in a cage, a fat bedraggled-looking green parrot with red and evil eyes, and this parrot, who was named Polly and shrieked a great deal, was to be featured quite a lot in future stories. Clara Trevlyn summed up the arrival of Bessie most aptly with these words:

'Bessie Bunter? Surely she isn't a relation of Billy Bunter — that fat boy at Greyfriars? Fat and shiny and conceited. I'm sure of it.'

In this story Bessie, like Billy, ran up a bill at Uncle Clegg's and — again like Billy — she had left her money at home, at Bunter Court. So Marjorie Hazeldene & Co had to pay what turned out to be only the first of many bills on behalf of the fat Bessie.

Meanwhile, Charles Down, who had taken over *The Magnet* and *Gem* from Pentelow, and was editor until the return of H.A. Hinton from war services, had become quite alarmed by the success of this new paper and, in his view, R.T. Eves had stolen his star author. Even with the departure of Pentelow to another paper, Frank Richards was still not sending in enough copy for Down's satisfaction.

Consequently, he went to the Director-in-Chief, then a Tod Anderson, and explained the position to him, and the outcome was that Frank Richards was given a strict set of priorities: (a) to supply Magnet stories (b) to supply Gem stories (c) to supply Rookwood stories. Stories for *School Friend* were nowhere. In other words, he was forbidden to write them. Either Reg Eves had to find new writers or the paper would simply have to close down.

To say that there was a panic in *The School Friend* office when this ruling was proclaimed would be an under-statement. However, a godsend was the fact that a *Boys Friend Library* Bessie Bunter story had not yet been used, and this was promptly carved into two and used in *The School Friend* as a stopgap until substitute stories could be written.

One must have considerable sympathy for Frank Richards who, after being particularly asked to launch a new paper with his own character creation was now forbidden to write for it and thereby denied a slice of his income.

On the other hand, he should have realised that he could not write a Greyfriars story (30,000 words), a St Jim's story (30,000 words) a Rookwood story (10,000 words) and Cedar Creek and other stories each week indefinitely.

These all added up to an output of over 100,000 words weekly and as he wrote chiefly in the morning, sometimes for a few hours in the afternoon, and almost never on Sunday it was a sheer impossibility for any one man.

In fact, in 1920, he wrote only nine St. Jim's stories for *The Gem* and only ten stories for *The Magnet* and eighty-five other stories consequently had to be written by substitute writers.

Editors seemed to have no idea whatsoever of the amount of copy a writer could turn out in a week, and the amount of work commissioned to Frank Richards at this time was once estimated as being enough to keep three full-time writers working night and day to maintain schedule.

Horace Phillips and Reginald Kirkham were brought in to continue the Cliff House stories, and their work was heavily edited to maintain continuity with the earlier tales. Phillips was a serious writer, whilst Kirkham was a very humorous one — evidence this essay from Bessie on the subject of a cat:

> 'The Catt walks and runns about. It playes with mouses. Little girls do not play with others and eat them. Catts stele food a lot. The catt is always taking food from my studdy. It robbes all the studdy's and I am blamed. I do not like catts for that reason and bekos they skrach.'

Significantly, after the first few issues a large number of girls wrote to the editorial offices complaining that Bessie was too fat, and many on the plump side complained of being tagged 'Bessie Bunter'. Reg Eves had made the initial assumption that girls were not psychologically different from boys. If Billy Bunter was a popular character so would be Bessie. The large number of readers who wrote in proved how

The Jester, 1ᵈ

And The Wonder.

No. 102.   EVERY SATURDAY.   OCTOBER 24, 1903.

GAWGE'S GENTLEMEN v. CHOLLY'S CHUMPS FOR THE TOOTSIE TROPHY.

KEEPER of the PIRATES' HOARD

by Charles Hamilton

Boy owner of the ketch Dawn, trading in the South Seas, Ken King is quite accustomed to finding himself in startling situations. Read now how he acquits himself in a pirates' headquarters!

The Dutchman was chuckling as he stared down at the wreck made by the dynamite. His chuckling changed to a gasp of terror as a strong grasp was placed on him from behind.

Face to Face!

KRELL, the Dutchman, peered from the loopholed palmwood shutter, smoking rifle in hand, and muttered gutturally in Dutch. High over the island sailed a silver crescent of moon, amid fleecy clouds, and silvery light fell on the sea, the beach, the bungalow in which he sheltered, the palm grove, and the steep hill behind.

But he could see nothing of the enemy who had chased him through the ravine from the other side of the island; nothing of the castaway whose life he had sought and from whom he had fled like a craven.

Every door, every window in the bungalow was fast. The Dutchman was armed with repeating rifle and revolver, and he knew that the castaway was armed only with a lawyer-cane. But his nerves were jumping as he peered from the loophole.

He had sighted Ken King, commonly known as King of the Islands, coming on from the palm grove, fired, and missed. He had had no second chance. The boy trader had dropped below the level of the coral platform on which the bungalow was built, and the bullets that Krell blazed away passed over him harmlessly.

If he rose and approached the bungalow—— But he did not rise. Krell dropped the butt of his rifle to the floor and wiped the perspiration from his brow. He shouted from the loophole :

COMPLETE IN THIS ISSUE.

"Wacht U op mij?" Then he remembered that Dutch was most likely a strange tongue to the castaway, and went on in beche-de-mer :

"You feller sailorman, you wait along me? You feller pig, you come along house belong me, s'pose you no flaid come along me."

King of the Islands, in cover under the edge of the platform, grinned. He was not likely to let the taunt draw him under the fire of the man who was watching for a chance to shoot him.

The Dutchman waited in vain for an answer from Ken.

The boy trader, keeping in cover, was planning his next step, and he was not in haste.

"You feller pig, you speak, mouth belong you!" shouted Krell. "What name you come along this house?"

"You feller Dutch pig," called back King of the Islands, speaking the beche-de-mer, which he guessed was the only English Krell knew, "what name you shoot feller gun along me? Plenty many time you shoot feller gun along me, along this island. What name you send feller nigger Pipaio along me, along feller knife? My word! Me comey along house killy feller Dussman plenty quick."

Bang! The rifle answered, the bullet whizzing over King of the Islands' head.

Ken laughed. The Dutchman had no chance of getting him unless he came out of the house. The edge of the coral platform was ten or twelve feet from the window whence Krell was firing, and without approaching

An Affair of State!
(A Grand School Tale of Tom Merry & Co. at St. Jim's.)

5,000 Prizes!
Your Last Chance this Week.

The GEM LIBRARY
1d.

No. 389. Vol. 9.

OH WHERE, OH WHERE IS GUSSY?
(A Screamingly Funny Incident in the Magnificent Complete School Tale inside.)

GORGEOUS TUCK HAMPERS FOR READERS!

The Greyfriars Herald

1½d

No. 12 (New Series). | FULL OF SCHOOL STORIES AND ARTICLES | Jan. 17, 1923.

MOBBING THE SLACKERS' ELEVEN!

false this assumption was.

When, later on, a story featuring a scholarship girl made an extraordinary hit, the circulation rose and *The School Friend* began to pay its way.

Reg Eves made no secret of his opinion that, whilst Frank Richards was the greatest writer for boys, his girls' stories were simply boys' stories with girls' names, and whilst Frank Richards quite forgave Down for halting his work in this field he resented Reg Eves for belittling that work.

One astonishing feature of the Cliff House stories was the complete absence of any mention of Greyfriars. It was felt that nothing was to be gained by using the school and that difficulties might arise unless there was close liaison between Cliff House and Greyfriars writers. On the other hand, Bessie Bunter still appeared in *The Magnet* right up to the end of the saga in 1940.

An unhappy conclusion must be recorded to the Bessie Bunter story, and it concerns John W. Wheway, who wrote well over 500 Cliff House stories between 1931 and 1940. Some years ago a well-meaning publisher advertised him as 'The author of the Bessie Bunter stories' and this called forth an almost vitriolic, completely uncharacteristic letter from Frank Richards. It accused Johnny Wheway, among other things, of being an impostor and of cashing in on Richards' own popularity by using his 'Hilda Richards' pen-name.

Being the mildest of men this upset Wheway a great deal as he only wrote the stories to editorial direction. A great admirer of Frank Richards from boyhood days when he had read *The Magnet* and *Gem* this experience changed his opinion of the great man completely and he was prompted to write the true facts in his own autobiography. However, like Mr Quelch's *History of Greyfriars* this was fated to remain unfinished. After a short spell in the editorial offices of Howard Baker Publishers in Bloomsbury he went into retirement and died in 1973.

Passionately jealous of his own creations, Frank Richards could see only one side of the picture and, throughout, Wheway remained, for him, the villain of the piece.

CHAPTER SEVEN

the question of substitution

Editors are notoriously harassed men, and none more so than those who launch boys' papers. Here the occupational hazards are truly horrendous. Forecasting the future of a boys' paper is even more difficult than backing racehorses to win, as the form book is no guide at all. Some have flourished unjustifiably, like the sinner and the green bay tree, whilst rivals of equal or superior merit perished while still in swaddling clothes.

The Amalgamated Press, with its multiplicity of papers, could afford to nurse and advertise its bantlings on a scale impossible to the smaller publishers. However, once the initial flush of youthful success was over, even the path of the Amalgamated Press was littered with calamity. Percy Griffith, then, by dedicating himself to St. Jim's had scored a major success and had every reason to feel pleased with himself.

But it was pleasure that could not last. For it took only the passage of a few weeks for Percy to realise that, in addition to the usual problems attending such a paper, he had a brand-new Damoclean peril hanging over his head.

In any ordinary paper of varied authorship the defection, illness or even death of one writer was of small account. In the extreme case, where an author died in the middle of writing a serial, other hands would contrive to finish the tale so expeditiously that no reader would even notice the difference.

But Percy Griffith now realised that in *The Gem* he had something else: a valuable property which could be virtually rendered worthless overnight if anything were to happen to the one man on whom its distinctive style and runaway popularity depended.

And when *The Magnet* was added to the Amalgamated Press list eleven months later the situation became even more acute. Now Griffith really did feel that he was living on borrowed time. No single author had ever tackled the responsibility of filling two whole papers before, and the editor must have wondered how long it would be before his pair of sweet money-spinners ran out of copy.

There was no sign of if yet: Frank Richards was not only meeting his obligations to the Companion Papers, he was also supplying Messrs Trapps Holmes and others with a never-ending stream of long complete stories and serials. But it couldn't go on for ever — could it?

Griffith knew that the heavy demands made upon Frank Richards meant that no stock-piling of stories was possible. *The Gem* and *Magnet* reserves were too slender for any complacency, and under the most favourable circumstances did not amount to more than three of four weeks' supply of material in hand. Nor did the most favourable circumstances always have to apply.

Griffith knew that there was only one thing to do, and he did it. He took out a practical insurance policy by arranging for other writers to experiment in the art, craft and mystery of writing St. Jim's stories — and so precipitated a row which has rumbled on ever since.

Frank Richards' version of the beginning of the substitute question is vague to say the least. According to him it all began with the editor handing him a manuscript of a St. Jim's story and asking him to make it fit for publication in return for half his usual fee for an original story.

And Frank Richards agreed.

The story was called *The Terrible Three's Air Cruise* and had been written by Harry Harper, an expert on flying and one-time *Daily Mail* war correspondent, and no doubt our author was flattered that such a man should have read enough of Tom Merry & Co. to be able to write about them. It was a further tribute to the fascination of those cheerful youths that he should want to do so, and Frank Richards said 'yes'.

He clearly didn't appreciate what he was letting himself in for. Nor did he know that eight stories that he had not written had already appeared in *The Gem* under his by-line. H. Clarke Hooke had written one; C.M. Down, two, and Percy Griffith, five!

Incredibly, Frank Richards had obviously never bothered to so much as glance at the paper for long enough to spot a 'dud' story.

In time these substitutes became a flood until, finally, by the end of the run of *The Magnet* and *Gem* in 1939–40 nearly 35 different authors had written Greyfriars and St. Jim's stories.

Throughout all his career at the Amalgamated Press, Frank Richards had almost a mania about these 'duds', as he called them, and not long after *The Magnet* ceased publication in 1940 he wrote:

> 'Although it was rather a blow to me to sever my connection with the Amalgamated Press after so many years, it was an immense relief to get away from the substitute writers, which have been an incessant cause of worry and discord. I have had experience of a good many publishers: but only one of a publisher employing hack-writers to raid the work of a popular author, even to the extent of pinching his pen-name to cover up the imposture — and I hope and believe that that experience will never be repeated.'

Frank Richards put the blame squarely on Percy Griffith for instigating what he called 'the whole miserable business' of the substitute writers, and it is impossible not to sympathise with the author. At the same time it is quite clear that whomever the editor had been he would have been forced to take the very same decision. An insurance policy he would have to have.

And the essential importance of that decision was shown early, in *The Gem's* second year, when Frank Richards defaulted with copy no less than eight times! Clearly the paper had to be protected against such eventualities.

On the other hand, Frank Richards complained with justice that Martin Clifford was *his* pen-name, and St. Jim's his creation, and that both were as much his as the sovereigns in his pocket.

With rather less justification, he suggested that in the event of his not being able to turn in his promised weekly story Griffith should print other stories by other writers, and acknowledge as such.

To this the editor retorted that if a boy paid his money to read about Tom Merry he was entitled to get Tom Merry, and that it was neither good sense nor good business to turn The *Gem* into a mixed story weekly again on the occasions when it suited the author's convenience.

If the author had stood firm, the irresistible force meeting the immovable object would have either blasted the paper into oblivion or moved it into a field of shortish runs of different series — to everyone's loss. He did not, and so the rancour and bitterness went on throughout the whole of the Companion Papers' run, and the affair became almost an obsession with Frank Richards for the rest of his life.

Nelson Lee, that famous rival to Sexton Blake, was created by Maxwell Scott (Dr. J.W. Stanniforth). He had a serious disagreement with the editor of *Pluck* in 1896, who was inclined to drop him from the paper. Scott then moved over to Pearsons. Later, he was astonished to see a story of Nelson Lee by another writer in *Pluck*, and so he promptly wrote to the Amalgamated Press, to the very top, Alfred Harmsworth, explaining that he was the creator. He received a prompt apology from the great man, and in later years sold the copyright to the Amalgamated Press who thereupon brought out the very successful 70,000 word *Nelson Lee Library.*

Maxwell Scott was a busy doctor freelancing from Yorkshire, and without many personal contacts in Fleetway House, but he achieved this. Frank Richards had been in and out of the place for a dozen years, had worked for practically all the editors and was friendly with at least one director, Hamilton Edwards — and achieved nothing.

Maxwell Scott was very small fry compared with *The Magnet* and *Gem* writer, but he had resisted impertinent encroachment on his preserves and suffered nothing by it. Just why Frank Richards never followed his example in putting up a fight which, on the face of it, he could not lose, is only one of many mysterious aspects of this affair.

Why Frank Richards never employed a business manager, or agent, to look after his interests — especially when he was abroad for long periods — is another mystery. They could have guided him through these difficult years. He was a star author who could, by negotiation, have almost doubled his income.

A forceful agent would have charged the Amalgamated Press a royalty for the use of the characters and come to some agreement with all parties on how the stories were to be presented. As it was, Frank Richards got the rate paid to general, run-of-the mill authors, and some did better by bargaining — including Edwy Searles Brooks of the St. Franks tales in the *Nelson Lee Library*, who got more per story for writing far less.

But while the Amalgamated Press could be said to be unreasonable so, in some cases, could Frank Richards. What would have been the reaction of readers if, say, a tale had appeared one week by-lined C.M. Down or H. Clarke Hook? Even the name of Charles Hamilton would have put readers off, however good the story under that name might be. It would have been compared unfavourably with a 'Frank Richards' or 'Martin Clifford' story, and confidence would have been undermined. Certainly, if it had happened often — as often as substitute stories were, in fact, used — sales would have started to slip.

On the other hand, the Amalgamated Press was, in a way, misleading the public into thinking that they were always buying the work of a world-renowned and highly popular author when, on occasion, they were not.

When C.M. Down was appointed editor in 1921 he attempted to reach a solution to the problem that had caused so much dissension over the years, and Frank Richards was offered — and accepted — the sum of £3,000 in payment for any claim he possessed of copyright in the series or characters.

One must multiply this sum by at least ten times to reach today's values, and it was a good offer. And it was accepted. Neverthless, it didn't settle the question. Not entirely.

It may have settled it then. It may even have settled it through to the last issues of *The Magnet* and *The Gem* in 1939-40, but Frank Richards brought the subject up again later. He continued to attack the entire conception of the substitute story throughout all the post-war years up to the time of his death, and waxed very bitter about it. Yet he never once mentioned that the subject had been settled by agreement in 1921.

His plaint bore a reminiscent smack of Bunter's argument when Peter Todd refused to give up the study armchair: "He thinks it's his — just because he paid for it, you know."

Looked at from an adult point of view the substitute stories were, in the main, pretty poor stuff. Which is understandable. It is impossible for any writer to put himself completely into another author's skin. Further, it has recently been discovered that youths of seventeen were asked by editors to write stories to keep the papers going in the First World War, and that some stories were written in the trenches, in Flanders, under the very worst conditions.

In such circumstances ordinary standards of criticism must be suspended.

Without substitute stories there would have been no *Magnet* or *Gem* after 1914.

The genuine Martin Clifford wrote approximately two

thirds of all St. Jim's stories in *The Gem*. In *The Magnet* the proportion was far higher: Frank Richards writing 1380 out of a total of 1683 Greyfriars stories, which was a very high ration indeed. If one accepts editors' statements, substitute stories did not affect circulations much, and there were no shoals of angry letters received fulminating against them. In fact the average reader was not aware, at the time, that such a thing as a substitute story existed, though some may have wondered why one Martin Clifford or Frank Richards story was so very much better than another.

Investigation into the subject of substitute stories only began long after *The Magnet* and *Gem* had ceased publication, and when groups of old readers started to exchange information and collect back numbers, and the last word on the subject probably properly goes to G.R. Samways, a former chief sub-editor and prolific substitute writer. When criticised severely for one of his stories in *The Magnet* he tersely replied:

> 'Stories should be judged by the market they were aimed at. They should not be perused by pedantic adults as if they are rare works of Shakespeare or other Classical authors. I was told by Amalgamated Press editors to write them, and if I had not done so there would have been no *Magnet* or *Gem* for these very same readers to enjoy in future years.'

And that says it all.

CHAPTER EIGHT

the gay blades

"Yaas," his Lordship [Lord Mauleverer] nodded amiably. "You've sailed pretty near to the wind, Loder. Frightfully near! Plenty of evidence for Prout to sack you, or for a judge to send you to chokey, what?"

In years to come, Percy Griffith would be acknowledged as the wizard from Wales without whom the two greatest boys' papers in the world would have had no existence. But when he finally quit the offices of the old Amalgamated Press in 1911 he left behind a reputation that rivalled Herbert Vernon-Smith and Cecil Ponsonby at their worst.

He also succeeded in obtaining more loans from fellow members of the staff than Billy Bunter at his best, and his expected cheque always remained in the same state of limbo as William George Bunter's celebrated postal order.

Small, dark haired and with a fiery temper, Griffith had left his native Wales whilst still in his teens and headed for London, where he had soon landed a job with the brothers Harmsworth, who were busily building the publishing house that was soon to be the largest in the world — the Amalgamated Press.

By 1907, he had risen in rank until he was a top editor, and he revelled in that position. Like many small men given power he was something of a dictator, and he ruled the roost with an iron hand.

It is odd that a man like Frank Richards, who was gifted with great powers of description, should be so niggardly in what he tells us in his Autobiography about his colleagues in those days. It says something for the force of Griffith's personality, therefore, that he is the only one of the editors mentioned of whom we get anything like a clear picture.

There is, in fact, a much more complete picture of him in the autobiography than the majority of readers imagine. One chapter, *Vie de Boheme*, deals with a man who was a strange mixture of journalist and self-appointed Bohemian — a man identified only by the intials V.C.[1]

This man was, in fact, Percy Griffith.

By day an astute editor, Griffith spent his nights raking around what passed for Bohemia in Edwardian London, and eventually marred what promised to be a brilliant career with the entanglements in which his off-duty excursions involved him.

Apart from *The Magnet* and *Gem*, Percy had launched two further papers for which his star author had written the opening stories and then found the pace too hot to continue writing for four papers each week on top of all his other commitments. The first of these papers was *Boys Realm* (Football and Sports Library) commenced in 1909, featuring tales of Jack Noble & Co of Pelham School. No less than a dozen other well-known authors continued the series.

The second was a curious venture in 1910 entitled *The Empire Library*. This had an intended special appeal to colonial readers, and featured Gordon Gay & Co of Rylcombe Grammar School, near St. Jim's in Sussex. This school had already featured in *The Gem* stories, and practically all of its pupils came from the Empire.

Unfortunately for Percy Griffith, after a few stories by 'Prosper Howard' — yet another new name for our author — there had been a dispute, and consequently Hinton and C.M.

---

1   Frank Richards explained the initials by claiming that the man concerned was the person on whom the character of Vane Carter, in the Carcroft School stories was based. But the briefest of comparisons will show that this is unlikely. The real reason for the use of the initials, then, is unknown.

Down had been forced to write the rest of the stories themselves — and the *Empire Library* was doomed almost from the start.

Later, the original 'Prosper Howard' did write a full length tale of the school for *The Boys Friend Library* entitled *The School Under Canvas*.

Both *The Gem* and *The Magnet*, however, were hugely successful and Griffith's future seemed assured. But though he was a married man with a family he found the bright lights of London impossible to resist and began to live far above his means. Percy, like the ancient Israelites, yearned for the fleshpots, and he soon found himself in debt. Paying high rates of interest to numerous money-lenders, he had to resort to finding more and more spare cash from other sources — like tapping friends at the office. And in the actual pursuit of money, Percy, like Nimrod of old, was a mighty hunter.

Unfortunately, he wasn't exactly reliable when it came to paying loans back, and at last whenever colleagues spotted him in the corridors of Fleetway House they 'saw him not, but vanished quickly into the shadows'.

Finally, when Frank Richards refused to stand security for a large loan, Percy decided to make the big killing, and then head for pastures new. The story went round that his wife was seriously ill, and that he needed money to pay for a major operation. It was an appeal that no-one could refuse. The money rolled in, and even office boys were dunned for their hard-earned half-crowns. And then, at the end of it all, Percy 'suddenly, silently vanished away', and Fleetway House knew him no more.

It was reported that he had gone abroad, and a rumour went round some years later that he had been arrested on some unknown charge in Canada and was asking all his old friends to rally round once more. His old friends, alas, heeded him not. And after that there was silence.

However, in the early twenties an editor who had known him swore that he had seen him on the Embankment from the open upper deck of one of the old trams. He said that Percy was now grey-haired and seemingly down-and-out. Strange to think that impecunious Percy, whose financial life was such a shambles, was the man who launched the two most loved boys papers — the biggest money-spinners — of them all.

Percy Griffith's chief sub-editor, Herbert Allen Hinton, took over after his dramatic exit, and what a contrast he was in size to Percy! Hinton was built like a Greek God. He had been to a public school with Lord Rothermere, and had played rugger for Blackheath. He was nicknamed 'Trooper': whether because he looked like one, or swore like one, or because he was connected with the Kent Yeomanry not being clear.

Frank Richards claimed that George Figgins of St. Jim's was modelled on him, though the connection seems vague. Figgins, in the early days, was distinctly lanky and the subject of many quips from his School House rivals about his lack of calves. One sub-editor of the period said that he could never understand the Figgins analogy, and that the only character who bore any resemblance to Hinton was Larry Lascelles, the games master of Greyfriars.

Hinton proceeded to model himself on Hamilton Edwards' pattern of boosting the editor whenever possible, and one of his ideas was to insert in his papers fictitious letters supposedly sent him by imaginary readers. These attacked him for not being in the army, and he was supposed to have received enough white feathers to open a Red Indian head-dress factory. He hoped in this way to bestir his readers to rise full-bloodedly to his defence and thus bring some interest and controversy into the papers.

In the First World War, Lord Northcliffe arranged for certain key men on his staff at Fleetway House to be granted exemption from military service. Hinton was a Captain in the West Kent Yeomanry (Territorial) and one of those excused. Certainly there was no question of evasion or cowardice on his part, for he was the bravest of men. Once when a burly van-driver was ill-treating a horse because it was slow in pulling a full cart up Ludgate Hill, he jumped up, pulled the carter down from his dray, and gave him the thrashing of his life.

Hinton was also most fastidious in the matter of hygiene.

When asking about the war in the trenches, he was far more concerned with the vermin than with the shelling. When engaging an office boy, his first question was never "Is he capable?" but "Is he clean?"

To impress visitors, he kept a box of black cigars in his desk, but seldom smoked them since he was very keen on physical fitness.

Unlike Percy, he had no pretentions to being a writer, and even the complication of an ordinary letter was irksome to him. Eventually, in 1916, he was called to the colours and he fought with great distinction as a Captain in the Coldstream Guards.

On his return from war service he resumed his old position and all seemed well. Unfortunately, he had developed expensive tastes and like Percy Griffith soon found himself in difficulties.

One source of extra income open to him was that of writing substitute stories, and finding their creation a chore he devised an ingenious method of producing the best imitation Frank Richards' Greyfriars story it was possible to get. He simply took several old genuine Frank Richards' tales and cut them up, and then reassembled them into a new story using scissors and paste. The new story was entitled *Bunter's Baby*, and appeared in the summer of 1920, but it was basically *Harry Wharton's Ward*, which had originally appeared in 1909.

Unfortunately, he was bowled out by the excellent memory of an office boy named Edward C. Snow. Taking the story to the printers, Snow spotted where it had come from and, since he harboured a grudge against the editor for some reason he took the tale to higher authority. As a result Hinton left Fleetway House almost as quickly as Percy.

It was really ironic, since Hinton had given Snow his job in the first place because of the lad's phenomenal memory of all the Greyfriars and St. Jim's stories.

After his dismissal from Fleetway House, Hinton became associated with a new company and determined to use his experience in rivalling the papers that had for so long brought him his salary cheque. *School and Sport* was the result, and this paper first saw light of day on 17 December 1921, and was owned by Popular Publications Ltd, which was actually Hinton. Incredible as it may seem, he succeeded in getting Frank Richards to write for him. Richards' view was that there was room for everyone, and that *School and Sport* could carry on alongside the Amalgamated Press publications without causing upset.

But the Amalgamated Press certainly did not share that view, and took pains to warn their readers that *School and Sport* had nothing to do with them and was simply an inferior attempt to cash in on the popularity of *The Gem*. Hinton even circulated his old readers using a mailing list acquired during his service as a Fleetway House editor, and ended his letter with his familiar 'Your Editor' signature.

Frank Richards used a new pen-name for his stories in this new venture, that of 'Clifford Clive', and his two long serials featured a boy called Harry Nameless of St. Kit's. The theme had been previously used in his famous *Boys Friend Library* story *The Boy Without a Name*[2].

Praise was bountiful from Hinton on how well Frank Richards' stories were going, and everything was hearty and genial. Unfortunately, one thing was lacking, and that was payment. Finally, Frank Richards refused to write any more unless some money was forthcoming and Hinton promptly brought in E.R. Home-Gall, another prolific writer, to finish the series. He too, as he remarked in later years, received "not one penny for all my labours, and a gentleman of the public school and all."

School and Sport crashed, of course, and Frank Richards took it all philosophically. Non-payment meant he held the copyright of the stories, and so some were reprinted in *The Boys Friend Library* and others in *The Boys Friend*.

Percy Griffith had borrowed many hundreds of pounds from Frank Richards and never paid any of them back. Hinton, in a sense, had done worse, by taking one of Frank Richards' original stories and getting paid for it, and then by defaulting on payment for his contributions to *School and*

2   The theme, in fact, goes back even further, to a story in *The Gleam* in 1902 entitled *The Man Without a Name*.

Sport. Frank Richards took an extremely charitable view in both cases, and one must admire him for being calm and compassionate in circumstances in which he could so easily have been bitter and angry.

The eventual fate of Percy Griffith is unknown, though there was a rumour that he had died in the early thirties. Herbert Allen Hinton however died a most tragic death on New Years Day in 1945. At that time he was editor of the famous *Dalton's Weekly* and had also been editing a children's newspaper. Whilst on a train near Weybridge Station during the blackout, the train stopped outside the station and thinking he was stepping on to the platform he fell to his death down the embankment.

CHAPTER NINE

a new editor but – a rift in the lute

Frank Richards had always liked Charles Maurice Down. Even though our author was too aloof to speak to most sub-editors, he had always murmured a few kind words to Down when he was sitting in a corner of the Magnet/Gem offices in the early days of the papers.

And, for his part, Charles Down had always greatly admired Frank Richards. So when the editorial mantle fell on Down's shoulders all was calm and bright. The two men were to join a happy relationship for the next twenty years.

Born in Woolwich, but living most of his life in Harpenden, Down was the son of a J.P. and notable sportsman who had won many cups riding to hounds and in show jumping. Coming from a distinguished family, he had joined the Amalgamated Press straight from Public School around 1904.

Originally on *Pluck* and *Marvel*, he moved over to the Companion Papers when Percy Griffith started this new department, and consequently had the distinction of being associated with the very first *Gem* and *Magnet* and with the last.

Extremely modest, quiet and dignified, he was a far less forceful personality than his predecessors. Although lacking the athleticism of Hinton he was intellectually superior to him. And he brought something else to the job.

MEET BILLY BUNTER IN AN ENTIRELY NEW ROLE—INSIDE!

The Magnet 2ᴰ

Billy Bunter's
Own Paper

POST OFFICE

RICH AT LAST!

WORLD'S CHAMPION RACING MOTORIST WRITES WITHIN!

The MODERN BOY

EVERY MONDAY.
Week Ending May 4th, 1929.

No. 65.
Vol. 3.

2ᵈ

LIGHTING THE AIRMAN'S WAY! Special Article Inside.

TELEPHONE HARPENDEN 334

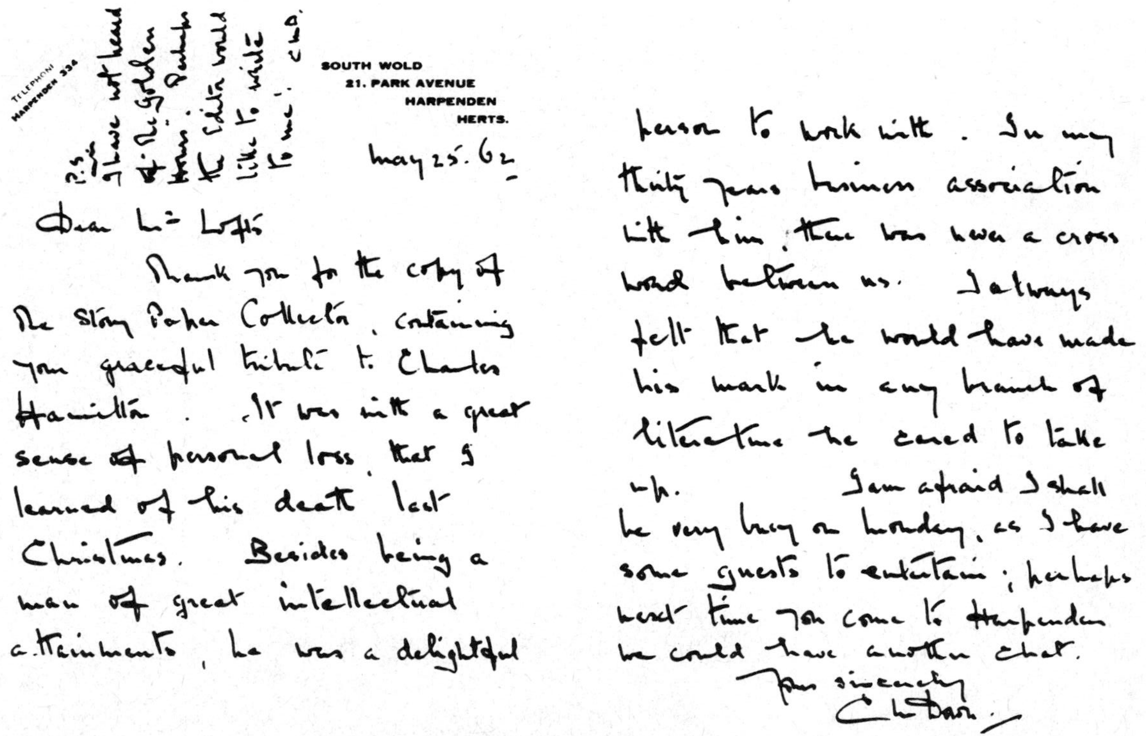

SOUTH WOLD
21. PARK AVENUE
HARPENDEN
HERTS.

May 25. 62

P.S. I have not heard of The Golden Hours. Perhaps the editor would like to write to me. C.H.D.

Dear Mr Lofts

Thank you for the copy of the Story Paper Collector, containing your graceful tribute to Charles Hamilton. It was with a great sense of personal loss that I learned of his death last Christmas. Besides being a man of great intellectual attainments, he was a delightful person to work with. In my thirty years business association with him, there was never a cross word between us. I always felt that he would have made his mark in any branch of literature he cared to take up.

I am afraid I shall be very busy on Monday, as I have some guests to entertain; perhaps next time you come to Harpenden we could have another chat.

Yours sincerely
C. M. Down.

Letter from Magnet editor on the death of Frank Richards

THE MAGNET "THE BOUNDER'S TRIUMPH!" Grand School and Detective-Adventure Yarn of Greyfriars

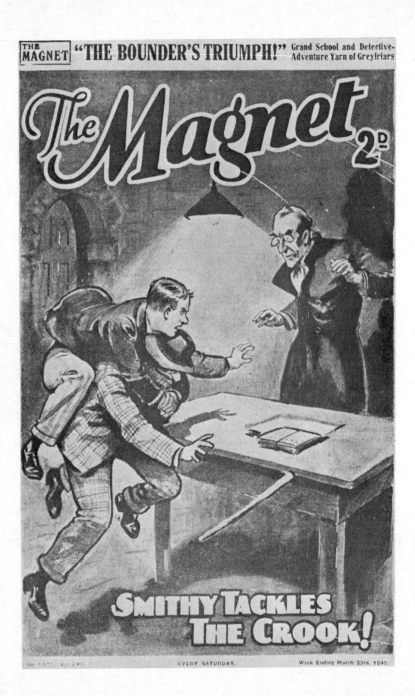

The Magnet

2^D

SMITHY TACKLES THE CROOK!

No. 1,677. Vol. LVII.   EVERY SATURDAY.   Week Ending March 23rd, 1940.

Unlike both Griffith and Hinton he had formed a great attachment to the characters in *The Magnet* and *Gem* and had written several stories nearer the author's style than any other writer. Indeed, a sub-editor, finding one of his St. Jim's stories in a drawer, thought at first it was by the genuine Martin Clifford. And this mistake has also been made by not a few experts in recent years.

Reminiscing on his days with *The Magnet* and *Gem*, C.M. Down has said:

> "From my first day of joining the staff I made a point of reading every Frank Richards manuscript that came into the office, and what a lot of pleasure I got out of the task. I became as familiar as I could with all of his characters — both in *The Magnet* and *Gem* — and there were quite a lot of them. And as I read more and more of the stories I came to have a great admiration for their author which continued long after the papers had finished. The passionate attachment of so many thousands of readers to the Companion Papers was never any mystery to me, as it was to some of my colleagues. It was inspired by the author's happy knack of projecting his own pleasant personality into his stories, through the characters he created.
>
> These characters made a lasting impression upon several generations of young people throughout the British Empire — and it is an impression that remains vivid to this day. St. Jim's, Greyfriars and Rookwood schools are still talked of familiarly by a large part of the adult population of this country."

Just before becoming full-time editor, one of Down's inspirations had been to suggest the publication of *The Holiday Annual* to the Amalgamated Press board of directors, and they had turned down the idea.

'If we have difficulty in getting boys to spend three pence a week on the Magnet and Gem (they were 1½d each in those days) *how on earth are they to be expected to find five shillings for an annual?'*

But they didn't, of course. Their parents did. And eventually persuasion won the day.

There was also the promise that new and novel-length stories would appear by all the three main authors — Frank Richards, Martin Clifford and Owen Conquest.

And so the first *Holiday Annual* appeared in the autumn of 1919, dated for 1920, and what a highly profitable venture that turned out to be! All 50,000 copies were sold long before Christmas, and the print order was doubled to 100,000 for succeeding years. It was one of the biggest money-spinners of them all.

Probably the most novel story that ever appeared was in the 1924 issue, when Martin Clifford visited Greyfriars. Some of the editorial staff thought that this story should not be published at all. Perpetuating the myth that the three famous writers were three different people, they held that it insulted the intelligence of their readership.

But the editorial policy was to keep the myth going, and so personal opinions were overruled.

A Great Man at Greyfriars gave an almost perfect description of Martin Clifford's style, written through the medium of William Wibley of the Greyfriars Remove by the great man himself:

> 'Some men write a story as if it were a furniture catalogue or an almanac. This man Clifford has an eye to a situation — he makes his characters explain themselves — before you've got a dozen lines into the story you know the fellows as if you'd met them.'

Another highly successful venture by C.M. Down was the *Schoolboys Own Library*, although the stories were nearly all reprints of earlier tales and were usually abridged. Perhaps the handy pocket size and the fact that boys could read them under a school desk undetected made them so popular. But whatever the reason, they enabled the reader to taste the best of the school stories that had been published in an earlier era.

Authors welcomed this Library as they were paid an honorarium of five guineas a story and were involved in no extra work. The required rewriting and cutting was done by the editorial staff — though not always as well as it might have been. One can gauge the popularity of the three schools when one learns that Greyfriars merited 184 stories in the Schoolboys Own Library, St. Jim's 81, and Rookwood 54. Indeed the sales of *The Magnet* were leaving *The Gem* well behind.

As revealed by Frank Richards, the lovable Arthur Augustus D'Arcy was principally based on the pleasant personality of C.M. Down, though other characteristics came from his own brother Douglas. Probably unknown to most readers, Frank Richards had created a double for Gussy in the *Aldine Diamond Library* at the school of St. John's — named after his own third Christian name. And even the pen name of 'Clifford Owen' has a familiar ring about it.

D'Arcy's double at St. John's was Marmaduke Percival Egbert Bly, son of a millionaire — all toppers, fags, and mannerisms such as 'Bai Jove, 'Yaas, wather', and 'Deah Boy'. But, after a few stories, Frank Richards found his other commitments too pressing to permit him to continue, and he ceased to write for the Aldine company. Instead, he concentrated on writing for the Amalgamated Press.

All was serene in the editorial offices of that company until one day in 1927 when, being in Town, Frank Richards spontaneously decided to call in at Fleetway House to discuss a new series for *The Gem*. The result was a rift in the lute which took a long time to mend.

For, not expecting his star author, Down was away from the office on business and had left his chief sub-editor to deal with any matters concerned with *The Magnet* and *Gem*. And Down and he could have not been more different.

The chief sub-editor in question was Hedley Percival Angelo O'Mant — to give him his full array of names. Irish on his father's side and Italian on his mother's, he was fairheaded and extremely good-looking. Still in his twenties, he was most popular with all of the staff and, in fact, no fewer than three secretaries in the department had fallen for his charm. He had married numbers one and three in the series, one at a time, of course, and quite legally since the Divorce Court had co-operated. Normally, one could not help liking Hedley.

He had a fine tenor voice and often sang at his work for, of course, he had cause to be happy. Extremely competent, he was of a younger generation than most of the editors at Fleetway House and was earmarked for future promotion to combat the ever-increasing threat of D.C. Thomson's intrusion into the juvenile periodical market.

O'Mant had briefly been an actor on the stage and had an artistic temperament. He was highly strung. This combined with his mixed ancestry made him, on occasion, very excitable indeed.

Eric Parker, the Sexton Blake artist who had an inborn knack of placing character perfectly, dubbed him 'Pin Wire'. Hedley, it must also be said, had no love or admiration for the characters of Greyfriars and St. Jim's. His own taste was for flying stories and when a youth of eighteen in the First World War he had flown planes when pilots had only a revolver to fight with.

Frank Richards had expected to see Maurice Down. Hedley O'Mant had not expected to see Frank Richards. And the plain fact was that they disliked each other on sight.

The outcome was a heated exchange, like Mr Quelch and Mr Prout having a Battle of the Beaks in the Masters' Common Room. The final result was that for the next four years Frank Richards' contributions to *The Gem* were few and far between.

The causes of the acrimonious outburst were past editorial decisions with which Frank Richards could not agree. The first concerned Ferrers Locke and his assistant, Jack Drake, who had appeared in short stories written by Hedley Scott — who, in fact, was O'Mant. Both of these characters were Frank Richards' own creations, and Jack Drake had had a somewhat well-travelled career[1].

1 In 1919, and in the new series of *The Greyfriars Herald* Frank Richards had written a series of school stories about St. Winifred's under the pen-name of Owen Conquest. In the course of these tales the school was evacuated, and Drake and his friend, Rodney, went on the *Benbow*, a Napoleonic warship anchored in a tributary of the Thames. After a series of adventures they were eventually sent to Greyfriars.

Unfortunately for Drake, he had to move again when his father could no longer afford the school fees, and so he became assistant to Ferrers Locke. Dick Rodney simply faded out of the Greyfriars stories, whilst the Ferrers Locke

The second grievance concerned plots for stories. It should be explained here that members of the staff of the Companion Papers were encouraged to think up plots for future stories in *The Magnet* and *Gem* for which, if accepted, they were paid a few guineas.

These plots were, of course, fully discussed by the editor and author, and adapted by the latter to suit his needs and his whim.

Frank Richards' output was vast. So vast that he simply had to have fresh ideas from other people – or he could easily have become very repetitive. He was committed to writing so many stories that he didn't have time to plot every detail in every one for himself. So this device was adopted, and it worked. And on a plot outline which could be written on the back of a postcard Frank Richards would hang any number of closely-packed, characterful pages, full of incident and his own special magic.

There are those who think that, in some way, this flawed Frank Richards' genius as a school-story writer and that he, alone, ought to have been able to think up every single plot that he ever used.

The answer to this is – did Shakespeare? And the answer to that question is: no.

There are others who account the plot skeleton as important as the fleshed out story hung upon it, and Hedley O'Mant was one of these. It is easy to understand why. O'Mant had supplied – through the editor – the basic idea for the famous Bunter Court series in *The Magnet* and also Angelo Lee, Airman, series in *The Gem*. Both series were highly successful, and Hedley was not slow in claiming a substantial share of the credit. Frank Richards heard of someone attempting to help himself to a part of the glory and, like the old Queen, was not amused.

Upon his return, C.M. Down was, of course, horrified that something had happened to upset his star author and did

detective tales were popular enough for them to be continued in *The Magnet*.

But after writing several stories Frank Richards either lost interest or found he could not fit yet another series into his already crowded schedule, and O'Mant took over. Frank Richards greatly resented this, and in later years accused O'Mant of "pinching" his characters, "lock, stock and barrel".

everything he could to try and smooth things over, but his task was a difficult one. O'Mant was too popular to be moved, and when he did change offices it was to take over *The Ranger*. But that was still some four years away.

Frank Richards was to write for *The Ranger* and for its successor, *The Pilot*, but he had to be induced to do so. And the man who worked that particular miracle was Controlling Editor Montague Haydon, who was to prove to Frank Richards that he was a very good friend in every sense of the word.

CHAPTER TEN

Bunter v Coker

One day in 1929, Frank Richards was somewhat astonished to be shown some copies of *The Thriller* containing a murder mystery serial by Edgar Wallace and to be told by C.M. Down, the editor of *The Magnet*, that he wanted a short series of Greyfriars stories on similar lines.

Nor was this all: in future Greyfriars stories he wanted Frank Richards to play down Bunter and to push Horace James Coker of the Fifth more to the fore.

Down was simply passing on the first instruction from a higher level. The second was his own idea, and in the nature of an experiment.

If all this left Frank Richards feeling slightly worried, the editor was even more so. Apart from the recent upset with Hedley O'Mant which had resulted in a dearth of stories from the real Martin Clifford, the sales of both Companion Papers had been slowly declining.

The Scottish firm of D.C. Thomson of Dundee had entered the juvenile field with *Wizard*, *Rover* and *Adventure* and had already drastically reduced the circulations of Amalgamated Press papers. Now rumour had it that they had other publications in the pipeline – including a school-story paper. Clearly something had to be done to halt *The Magnet's* decline.

Free gift schemes — always a sure sign of a paper's flagging popularity — were not the complete answer. At an editorial conference, Monty Haydon, Controlling Editor, had suggested that they could do worse than have a *Magnet* series on the lines of an Edgar Wallace murder mystery serial. Haydon's paper, *The Thriller,* which had been launched in February 1929, had proved to be a tremendous success. Although aimed at an older group of readers, he reasoned that perhaps boys, too, now wanted more meat in their stories.

Whether Frank Richards had ever read a murder mystery by Edgar Wallace is unknown, and the two men never met. But they were certainly alike in many ways.

Both were writers at the top of the tree in their respective fields, each having a prodigious output. Both were generous to a fault; both good hearted. And both had scant regard for money and usually gambled it away as fast as they earned it — the one on slow racehorses and the other on wrong numbers at the tables in Monte Carlo.

C.M. Down's preference for Coker over Bunter was not unusual, and the Fifth Former was well-liked by readers. Scarves, ties, socks and pullovers were sent to Coker regularly, care of the Amalgamated Press, by girl readers, whilst Bunter at best got jam tarts and cakes, and all too often they were joke cakes — made of soap!

The fact was that Bunter was detested by many of *The Magnet's* regular readers, even though he had developed over the years from being a short-sighted, stammering youth whose stock phrase was "I'm s-sincerely s-sorry" to being a much more sympathetic and characterful creation by the mid-1920s.

Frank Richards' absorption with Bunter gave the reader a unique schoolboy, but it had led to the Greyfriars stories being written to a formula.

That formula was simple: drag Bunter in at every opportunity and make the plot revolve around him. Any secret or tittle-tattle of news was known to Bunter, who either heard it from behind the sofa in the visitors' room or from behind a study armchair, or whilst hiding from some outraged Greyfriars boy whose tuck he had stolen.

Even outside the walls of the famous school no secret was safe. Bunter would be hiding behind a bush or up aloft in the groaning branches of a tree to overhear the dastardly plot.

Was there a schoolboy coming to the school by train, accompanied by a villain with evil or criminal intentions? There was Bunter again, of course, hiding under the carriage seat, listening to their scheming and with only a platform ticket or bent French penny to his name.

Billy Bunter simply overflowed into the stories. He had his finger in every pie, real or metaphorical, and was thus part and parcel of every story.

Horace James Coker, likewise, had developed from a minor, rather mild character into a fool like Bunter, but a decidedly more credible one. He was often used to further a plot when not playing a star part in it, and he had the enormous advantage over Bunter of not being totally unrealistic. He was absolutely honest, brave and generous, and one could not help liking him, despite his buffoonery and overbearing ways. He was also pig-headed and stubborn. One does find Cokers in all walks of life — but never a Bunter.

And just as Coker was liked, so were his so-called friends William Potter and George Green disliked by readers. "I will be your true friend," wrote one girl reader. "You are worth far more than your *scrounger* friends."

Scroungers they truly were, of the highest order; their regard for Coker being nothing more than a vested interest in his generosity, free holidays and, of course, Aunt Judy's large food hampers.

And so in obedience to the edict handed down from Monty Haydon the Ravenspur Grange series was written for the summer holidays of 1929 (*Magnets* 1122—1125). This series was actually an offshoot of what was known as 'The Trike Series'[1], the four preceding numbers (1118—1121). In this there was an ancient motor tricycle nicknamed Methuselah, and in issue number 1121 Billy Bunter sold the

---

1 Frank Richards thoroughly enjoyed writing 'The Trike Series' as he had always been a keen cyclist and had been a member of the Italian Cyclist's Touring Club in Italy in 1914.

machine to Gunner of Rookwood, and then fled in haste to escape the wrath of Bob Cherry. In consequence he conveniently disappeared from the next four stories and from the series built around Ravenspur Grange.

The Ravenspur series is extremely readable, but whether Frank Richards was happy about writing it is debateable. Readers who liked thrillers no doubt enjoyed it, but others who were not so steeped in the genre didn't care for the series and thought that four murders, one after the other, should never have occurred in *The Magnet*.

But, of course, the main cause of concern was that Frank Richards had taken his editor's instructions seriously, and Bunter was completely absent from the stories.

Those who disliked Bunter, naturally, rejoiced, whilst those who were fond of the Fat Owl uncharacteristically now put pen to paper. The silent majority was silent no more, and The Magnet office soon learned from shoals of letters that swiftly poured in who was the most popular character.

Many, indeed, threatened to stop having the paper unless he returned to the stories, and so both experiments failed, and Bunter was quickly restored.

But perhaps because of this brief interlude one did get some really classic Coker stories in this period and for years afterwards, including the famous Caffyn series (1404—12). So readers may have something to thank C.M. Down for after all. And it is certainly a fact that in post-war years Frank Richards — who had a soft spot for Coker and didn't mind pushing him at all — went on record as saying that the funniest story he ever wrote was *The Boy Who Wouldn't Be Caned* (Magnet No. 1042, 1928) and this, of course, featured Horace Coker.

In the early thirties, with Frank Richards writing almost every *Magnet* issue, substitute stories were rare. Even if submitted they were usually rejected for one reason or another. It is amusing to note, however, that a writer named Michael Duffy, probably in the knowledge that the editor had a soft spot for Coker, wrote a story entitled *Coker on the Dirt-Track*.

This was accepted by C.M. Down and published as

Speedway Coker (No. 1220, 1931) and was the very last substitute story to appear in *The Magnet*.

All the rest of the stories published, right down to the day on which the paper finally ceased publication, came from the pen of the genuine Frank Richards.

CHAPTER ELEVEN

friends and foes

Frank Richards had only the slenderest link with the editorial staffs of the papers for which he wrote. His appearances at Fleetway House were 'like angel visits, few and far between', and he was as ignorant of the Companion Papers' administrative team as they were of the great writer whose stories passed through their hands.

His manuscripts in their immaculate typescript were always addressed to the editor with the briefest of covering notes. The author knew little and cared less about the inner workings of the papers. He scarcely ever alluded, in speech or in writing, to the staff of the papers, and when he did do so, much later on, it was in terms of amused contempt. 'The Menagerie' was his pet name for the offices and staff.

Why he should have adopted this attitude, and also evidenced such a dislike for editorial conferences, is not at all clear. But it could have stemmed from his Trapps Holmes days, when he was asked to write half a dozen stories of a certain length and then left to get on with it. He had a completely free hand. The Amalgamated Press being more methodical and businesslike insisted on an author discussing future themes for stories with the editors of the papers concerned, and it may be that it was this which made Frank Richards contemptuously impatient.

In any event, as he bluntly revealed in his Autobiography, he spent his conferences with Percy Griffith day-dreaming most of the time: either making up chess-problems or mentally reciting poems to himself. This may have sounded amusing to the reader, but must have been very galling to the editor when he discovered that his reasoned discourse had been all for nothing and his creative ideas were simply ignored.

In his early days, our author visited Carmelite House twice a week, later reduced to a single weekly visit when he had to travel from his seaside cottage. Later still, his travels abroad made his visits more infrequent, until there would sometimes be months between them. Again later, and when his 'gammy' leg[1] was playing him up, C.M. Down had to travel down to Kent to see him.

George Richmond Samways, a chief sub-editor, relates how he once met Frank Richards on one of his rare visits to Fleetway House:

> "It was mid-afternoon, I remember, when a brown-uniformed messenger girl tapped at the door of Room 59, opened it in response to Hinton's call, and announced: "Mr Hamilton, sir!"
>
> Hinton sprang to his feet and greeted the distinguished visitor with the greatest cordiality. He relieved him of hat and coat and piloted him to the large comfortable armchair reserved for callers. He briefly introduced me to the famous visitor. A box of cigars was then produced and the editor and his star author plunged into their business. It related to the launching of a new series of stories which was badly needed to boost a boys' paper.
>
> Charles Hamilton would then have been about forty, or so it seemed to me, and at the height of his powers. I confess I was disappointed in my idol. He seemed quite an ordinary and nondescript little man — an almost colourless personality — though it is but fair to say that most men would have

1 After the Second World War, in a merry quip — a jibe at his enemy the Amalgamated Press — Frank Richards called this his 'A.P. leg' — "because it always lets me down".

appeared ordinary and nondescript and colourless beside Herbert Alan Hinton, a man of magnificent physique, and as handsome as Apollo. In the overpowering presence of this Olympian, lesser mortals seemed visibly to shrink, and Charles Hamilton was no exception.

Yet, although the physical giant might dwarf and dominate the little man in the armchair, that little man was undoubtedly the intellectual superior, and as such he commanded my attention and respect. He addressed me once or twice, it is true, but I think we were a little nervous of each other: and the entrance of the office boy with a tray of tea provided a welcome diversion.

Charles Hamilton stayed a little longer. A cordial handshake with Hinton, a brief nod to me, and the great man was gone."

Frank Richards did however make friends through his brief visits to Fleetway House, and probably the first was Sydney Clarke Hook, nephew of Theodore Hook, the eighteenth century dramatist and novelist. Black-bearded Hook was, like Richards, a great traveller, well educated, and an expert on languages. In all probability they met frequently abroad.

Hook had the distinction of writing the very first boys' story for the Harmsworth Brothers in the *Halfpenny Marvel* way back in 1893, and shortly afterwards his world-famous characters of Jack, Sam and Pete delighted several generations of readers. Frank Richards said about him:

"I knew Clarke Hook very well indeed. He was a most charming cultured gentleman, and I once introduced his famous and delightful characters in an early St. Jim's story — when Tom Merry was in London."

Clarke Hook's son, Herbert, was also a school story writer — 'Ross Harvey' — and quite a good one, but unfortunately he did not rank as high as his father in our author's esteem. He was the writer of some of the early St. Jim's and Greyfriars substitute stories and Frank Richards' terse comment was "He was one of those wretched impostors".

Possibly one of Frank Richards' closest friendships was

with Clive Robert Fenn, son of the distinguished Victorian boys' writer George Manville Fenn. Clive Fenn had tried his hand at writing stories, but none had the same impact as his father's, and so he had obtained a position answering readers' letters in Room 60 at Fleetway House.

Fenn was a very quiet, unobtrusive sort of man, keeping very much to himself.

The mushroom growth of *The Magnet* correspondence soon made it impossible for every letter to be answered in the columns of the paper. A great many of the letters were therefore replied to by post, and it was Clive Fenn's job to tap away at his typewriter all day, surrounded by reference books, answering some of the more difficult questions from readers.

Letters poured in from all parts of the world — from readers wanting back-numbers of *The Magnet* and *Gem*, from other readers wanting pen-friends, or to meet Harry Wharton, or asking exactly where the schools were situated.

Why did Harry Wharton and Tom Merry never grow up? Would Frank Richards please send a cricket team to Yorkshire — or Cornwall — to play the local team? Could someone make a date with Marjorie Hazeldene, to take her to the pictures?

Many letters were actually addressed to Greyfriars School, Friardale, Kent, and these were forwarded on to Fleetway House by the postal authorities. Letters addressed to Frank Richards were usually answered by Clive Fenn or the editor, but in certain cases, where it was deemed important enough for the author himself to reply, the letter was sent on from Fleetway House.

Whether Frank Richards made friends with Clive Fenn through this medium, or whether it was as a result of his admiration for his father is not known, but the two men formed a lifelong friendship which was only broken when Fenn died at Bognor Regis in 1953.

Before that, Frank Richards was to make an odd claim: that his friend Clive Fenn was the best of the substitute writers!

But it wasn't true.

On being approached about this, Fenn replied rather bitterly "No, I never wrote any at all. The only story I ever attempted was rejected by John Nix Pentelow, the editor. He then proceeded to carve six stories out of my original plot." W. Stanton Hope seems to have been the only author who had some sort of collaboration with Frank Richards, as he often used to talk of their views on the various series. He would also yarn on the merits of the Rio Kid stories, and made the revelation that "we decided that the Herlock Sholmes series was not remunerative enough, and so we dropped them".

When Stanton Hope first met Frank Richards is not clear, but it was probably when he was chief sub-editor on the comic *Chuckles* and they were running short Greyfriars stories about the time of the First World War. Son of a well-to-do publishing family, he served in the Army with C.M. Down at Gallipoli. On his return, he was on *The Popular* and *Boys' Herald* papers before going freelance. A world-wide traveller, he wrote his autobiography *Rolling Round the World for Fun* in 1925, and later started the Stanton Hope College of Journalism in Australia. He was also a writer on technical subjects and well regarded in this field.

He married for the second time late in life, and he and his young wife visited Frank Richards at his home at Kingsgate just before leaving for Australia. He died in Sydney, in 1961, at the age of 72.

Frank Richards was basically a very friendly man, but as has been remarked his attitude towards substitute writers was uncompromisingly antagonistic. It is thus rather astonishing that he always spoke in glowing terms about S. Clarke Hook (who had written a St. Jim's story in an early *Boys Friend Library*), W. Stanton Hope, and the three editors, Griffith, Hinton and Down.

All the latter four gentlemen wrote stories of his creations, yet it is possible that he did not know about it. They, for their part, thought it tactful not to mention the fact. Around 1955, a substitute writer named Fred Gordon Cook wrote to

By arrangement with H. M. TENNENT LTD.
and LINNIT & DUNFEE LTD.

CITY STAGE PRODUCTIONS LTD.

present

BILLY BUNTER'S CHRISTMAS CIRCUS

By MAURICE McLOUGHLIN

and the Executors of the late FRANK RICHARDS, Creator of "Billy Bunter".

Characters in order of appearance :

William George Bunter ...	...PETER BRIDGMONT
Bob Cherry ...	PETER SANDERS
Johnny Bull ...	DAVID GRIFFIN
Harry Wharton ...	GREGORY WARWICK
Frank Nugent ...	BARRY HENDERSON
Hurree Ramset Jam Singh (Inky)...	LOUIS AQUILINA
Mr. Quelch (the Remove Form Master)...	ROBERT LANKESHEER
Fred (a General Utility Man) ...	JOE GREIG
Capt. Enrico Borrelli (the Ringmaster) ...	ROBERT BOND
Sonia (his Step-daughter)...	BERNADETTE MILNES
Carlo (a Clown) ...	MICHAEL ANTHONY
Mungo ...	A GORILLA

Directed by RICHARD DALE

Settings designed by JOHN BARRY

First Performance : Monday, 24th December, 1962

SYNOPSIS OF SCENES

SCENE 1   A CORNER OF THE GYM, AT GREYFRIARS SCHOOL. END OF CHRISTMAS TERM.

SCENE 2   THE PLATFORM AT FRIARDALE STATION. A FEW DAYS BEFORE CHRISTMAS.

SCENE 3   THE PARK AT WHARTON LODGE, WHERE THE ENTRANCE TO THE CIRCUS IS BEING ERECTED.

INTERVAL

SCENE 4   INSIDE THE CIRCUS TENT.

SCENE 5   THE SAME. LATER THAT NIGHT.

At the Piano : ERIC FAYNE

Selection of Billy Bunter music composed by Eric Fayne

Scenery built and painted by Robert Lister Studios.
Costumes by Morris Angel & Son. Knitwear by Marks & Spencer.
Harvest Cakes and Jam Tarts by Lyons Bakeries. Property foods by Pytram Ltd.
Cigarettes and Cigars by Abdulla & Co. R. J. Freeman & Son.
Boys' Primsalls by North British Rubber Co. Property Fish by Mac Fisheries.
Ironing by Hoover. Trolley by Alfred Allen & Son. Bowlers by Hyam & Co.
Rupidahave by Colgate-Palmolive. Blue Label bananas by Elders and Fyffes.
Boys' shirts and sports shirts by Daniel Neal. Coca-Cola by Coca-Cola Southern Bottlers Ltd.
Stalls' Ball by Tirum. Shoe Care by Tuxan Ltd. Wardrobe care by Lux.

For CITY STAGE PRODUCTIONS LTD.:

Production Manager ...	DAVID STEWART
Company and Stage Manager ...	ERNEST WOODFORD
Deputy Stage Manager ...	JERRY BARBOUR
Assistant Stage Managers ...	JACKIE WILLOWS
	KATHLEEN BROWNLIE
Wardrobe Mistress ...	MICHAEL MACMANUS
Press Representative ...	JOHN MAHONEY (MUS 8873)

House Manager (for the Queen's Theatre) ... REGINALD GOSSE

Box Office (NORMAN JOHNSON) open 1 a.m.-8 p.m.; REG 1166

The Management reserve the right to refuse admission, also to make any alteration in the cast which may be tendered necessary by illness or other unavoidable causes.

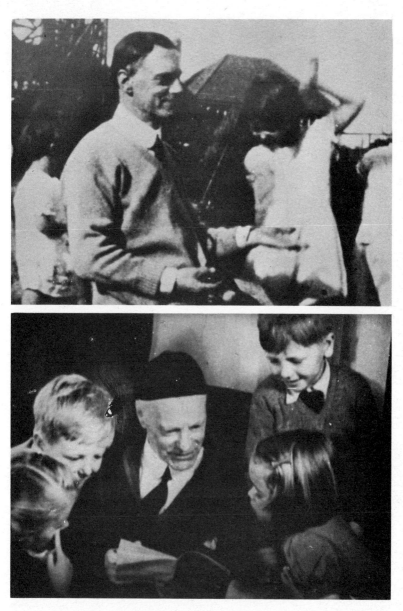

Top: A youngish "Frank Richards" at
      childrens garden party in the late twenties.
Bottom: An elderly "Frank Richards" reading
      a Greyfriars story to young listeners.
Photo's: The Charles Hamilton Museum.

Photo's: The Charles Hamilton Museum.

Frank Richards expressing his pleasure that the author was still hale and hearty. He also mentioned that he had written a few St. Jim's and Greyfriars stories himself. Frank Richards did not reply.

Later, in correspondence, he said: "I had, the other day, a letter from one of those wretched impostors. It completely spoiled my day. Why they did those things I cannot understand . . ."

Frank Richards certainly had his firm friends and his declared foes, and the staff of the Amalgamated Press must have been very puzzled indeed from time to time, down the years, as to which category they belonged.

CHAPTER TWELVE

the fleetway artists

If Frank Richards showed little interest in the editorial staff of the papers he wrote for, he had an almost lamentable lack of knowledge of the artists who illustrated his stories.

One can only conclude that either he never studied copies of his own tales, or else that he simply ignored the existence of any artist he did not like.

When Leonard Shields died in 1949, the newspapers made quite a splash with a headline — *Bunter Artist Leaves £67,902* — which prompted Frank Richards to write to the *Sunday Express*:

> "Mr Leonard Shields, who left £67,902 did not create Billy Bunter, even as an artist. He was the creator, as artist, of my other character, Bessie Bunter. The character of Billy Bunter in *The Magnet* was created by me as author and by Arthur Clarke as artist. Whether Mr Shields was one of the many artists who drew Billy Bunter after Arthur Clarke's death I do not know . . . It is good news that the artist was able to save 'thousands'. He had better luck than the author, who is still under the necessity of kicking for a livelihood at getting on for eighty."

It was unfortunate that this letter was ever written, and not only because of its somewhat peevish and ungraceful tone, which must have prompted many to speculate that perhaps the artist had shown more sense in the way he had handled his cash than had the better-paid author.

Worse — Frank Richards was all at sea with his facts. Arthur Clarke was not the original illustrator of *The Magnet*, as many of the former readers could have told him — and did. The artist for the first thirty-nine issues was Hutton Mitchell.

Mitchell could have had the job indefinitely, but he was always late with his drawings, and at length the editor just could not stand the delays any longer. Mitchell was a very swift worker and could dash off a set of pen-and-ink drawings in a remarkably short time, but he would not start work until the very last moment — and sometimes after. He just would not get down to the steady grind demanded by the Amalgamated Press.

Mitchell's work also appeared in *The Gem* where, curiously, it was Arthur Clarke who illustrated the first twenty or so issues before eventually taking over the Greyfriars characters.

Bessie Bunter's illustrators, after C.M. Chapman had produced the first sketch in *The Magnet* were G.M. Dodshon and T. Laidler, both of whose work was to be found regularly in *The School Friend*.

Leonard Shields, who was born in Yorkshire, had the distinction of illustrating the original St. Jim's stories in *Pluck*, and from this date onward his work was very much sought after by editors. In his heyday he contributed illustrations to as many as a dozen papers weekly. His schoolgirl drawings were in the Morcove stories in the *Schoolgirls' Own* and *Library*.

It was not until 1926, and in the India series, that his work first appeared in *The Magnet*, helping out the regular artist C.H. Chapman. The two men soon became firm friends and collaborated in the illustrations. A fast worker, Shields could finish a *Magnet* cover in an hour, and was considered a better craftsman than Chapman.

Thrifty by nature, and always to be seen wearing an old naval jacket from the First World War and thick boots, he had his hair cropped short and was, like Fisher T. Fish, extremely careful with his money. Once, when a fellow artist succeeded in selling him a threepenny raffle ticket it was the talk of Fleetway House for days after.

Shields had also been left several legacies, and by shrewd investment had gradually built up a fortune. But it should also be said that he was a very good sort, well liked by his fellow artists, and that he worked hard and earned a good income.

Taking all of this into account, the facts were that at the end of all of his labours his income was still only about half that of Frank Richards, and out of this he had a wife and children to support.

In later life he became crippled with arthritis in his hands, a dreadful fate for any artist. But he still attempted to sketch the boys of Greyfriars at his drawing board. Although in great pain and difficulty he never complained. He died in 1949, aged 72.

Frank Richards met C.H. Chapman for the first time around 1912 when he actually bumped into him in *The Magnet* office, but both being small men no harm was done. Richards had several suitcases with him, and was obviously just off on a trip abroad. The two were introduced and got on famously, and always spoke in glowing terms about each other after this first meeting.

C.H. Chapman had been brought in hurriedly after Arthur Clarke had died suddenly whilst actually at work on an illustration for *The Magnet*, and was a far better artist than Hutton Mitchell.

His strict instructions were to copy Clarke's style, so his natural talent was curbed for the first few years. So well did he copy Clarke that few were aware of any change of artist.

Later, as time went on, the change did become more apparent, and his work was distinguished by a definite angularity in his human subjects. He was clever with landscapes and rugged seascapes, and almost brilliant in his treatment of horses, which he greatly loved.

The illustrations of the individual boys at Greyfriars did eventually reach the stage where the reader could distinguish one from another — this apart from the obviously fat Bunter and the matchstick Todd cousins. It was Chapman who first put Bunter into checked trousers to distinguish him from Johnny Bull, and one could easily identify Herbert Vernon-Smith with his lean, well-dressed frame, striped trousers, and hard features.

Heavier Johnny Bull had a pug face and large mop of black hair, happy Bob Cherry had fair, curly hair and a cheery expression, whilst Harry Wharton was staid and serious and rarely smiled. Harold Skinner was skinny, and Horace James Coker of the Fifth had a large, pudding face. Soon the characters were almost drawing themselves.

Chapman's Bunter was the Fat Owl of the Remove that everyone knew, and in fact Chapman's pictures of Greyfriars and its schoolboys are the ones that most readers remember. Unlike other artists who had to work to the editor's instructions, he used to take the original Frank Richards' manuscripts home with him and made his own selection of scenes to illustrate.

In the nineteen twenties, when substitute stories were common, he would often produce covers months in advance. These would illustrate some purely imaginary incident that he had dreamed up himself[1] and a substitute writer would be told to write a story around it.

C.H. Chapman lived practically all of his life in the Reading area of Berkshire. Married, with six children, he was a staunch Churchman and a very keen cyclist. Friendly and generous, he gave away hundreds of his original drawings in the post-war years and travelled long distances — even when he was nearly ninety — to give talks on his work which he would illustrate, on a blackboard, with continuing consummate skill.

His closer friendship with Frank Richards did not really develop until *The Magnet* had long since ceased publication and both of them had become famous, as the illustrator and the writer of the Greyfriars stories. Both men were, of course, roughly the same age: both were religious, and both fond of cycling.

1   One was of Coker riding a motor-bike.

Very little is known about R.J. MacDonald except that he was a Scot and that after a number of artists had illustrated *The Gem* he took over and became the pre-eminent St. Jim's illustrator.

Whilst he was absent during the First World War the great Warwick Reynolds took over. One uses the word 'great' simply because Reynolds was far superior to any other Companion Papers' artist, and his animal drawings in later years became quite famous. When word got around that an original Reynolds illustration was being returned from the printers, staff, it is said, used to queue outside the editor's door in the hope of obtaining it. An original Reynolds painting of Tom Merry hung in a Fleetway House office for over forty years and the editor refused countless extravagant offers for it.

R.J. MacDonald, who lived at Lymington and owned a yacht, was possibly on friendlier terms with Frank Richards than Chapman since — probably at the author's suggestion — he was invited to illustrate the very first Bunter books of the post war years. Public opinion and readers' letters soon worked the oracle, however, and C.H. Chapman, Bunter's best illustrator, was brought back to work.

Frank Richards never mentioned Warwick Reynolds, Hutton Mitchell or Leonard Shields at all to our knowledge, except to comment in envious tones on Shields' good fortune. Nor did he have anything to say about the Rookwood illustrator, G.W. Wakefield, either, unless he did so in private correspondence.

However, C.H. Chapman mentioned the Rookwood artist — and in terms of anger!

When Phillip Hayward had ceased to illustrate, he and Wakefield were asked for an interview in the *Boys Friend* office. Chapman was there first, but it did him no good. The huge Wakefield just pushed past him — and got the job!

CHAPTER THIRTEEN

home life at Rose Lawn

As far as work was concerned, 1920 saw Frank Richards riding the crest of the wave. By now he was earning sums of money which were the envy of his contemporaries, was prosperous, and untrammelled by financial worries. Money had come through his sheer ability to turn out story after story for an ever-mounting number of editors eager for the boost that Richards' work alone could give them.

No longer did he have to grope for a market as in those far off days when competition was fierce. His problem, if indeed he ever considered it as one, was to satisfy his literary commitments with stories woven around the characters which he insisted were his alone.

Whether he had maintained quality of output as well as quantity throughout all the years leading up to his success is questionable. But the best was yet to come. Ahead lay the truly great series packed with a depth of characterisation as yet unseen, and invested with an air of tranquillity. Even in stories of near-tragedy the reader knew beyond doubt that there would be a serene conclusion.

This air of tranquillity emanated from Frank Richards himself: from his confidence in the knowledge that his income was secure whilst he virtually held the future of the Amalgamated Press's juvenile department in the hollow of his hand, and from something else: it came from the peaceful new surroundings he had found for himself.

In the early days, he had frequently caused his editors not a few headaches and not a little sweat when the deadline for publication came round and his manuscript was conspicuous by its absence. Much of this was due to his insatiable urge to travel which had involved extended trips to the Continent.

More than once he had conscientiously done his stint for his editor only to have his good intentions upset by insuperable difficulties in delivering his manuscript. He did his best. He had even travelled the Alps with a typewriter strapped on each side of a donkey — he was rarely without a spare machine. In Austria in 1914 every story he wrote was censored and sent to London in two parts, and one story concerned a Zeppelin. This was actually passed by the censor, but the second part reached London considerably ahead of the first — and thereby caused the editor a few grey hairs.

When the Great War broke out Frank Richards' feet ceased to itch. They had to in wartime; there was little alternative. On his return to England he spent his first night home at the village of Hawkinge — shades of Tom Redwing — a charming little village situated between Folkestone and Dover. And it was in Hawkinge that he first made the acquaintance of Miss Edith Hood, then a young child of nine years, who was fated to be associated with him for a considerable part of his life.

At first he stayed in lodgings over the Post Office in Hawkinge village, and he found the area most attractive despite the large number of military personnel in the vicinity.

For a time he involved himself in a certain amount of commuting between Hawkinge, Hampstead Garden Suburb and Buckinghamshire, where he had a cottage, but with the ending of the war he made up his mind. First, he took Clyde Cottage in Hawkinge, with Mrs Beverage, his housekeeper, to run it for him. Then, in 1921, he had a bungalow built to his requirements. Several miles outside the village, it was small and sheltered and lit by oil lamps, with paraffin for heating and cooking. Water was drawn from a well. An abundance of fruit trees around it quite naturally gave rise to the name 'Apple Trees' — and so he named it. It was a fine retreat, a veritable haven in which to escape all unwanted attention.

Continuing his acquaintanceship with the young Miss Hood, she became on his invitation the nursemaid to his sister's child, Una, then living at Sandgate and the apple of his eye. It had been a great moment of joy in his life when his niece had been born, and he adored her as most bachelor uncles do their young nieces.

Late in 1925 he took the step that was to inspire the very best of his material. This was when he purchased 'Rose Lawn', a neat white-walled house situated at Kingsgate-on-Sea in a quiet thoroughfare named Percy Avenue. A more delightful place it would be hard to find. At the end of the road was the North Foreland where the sea could be seen in all its glory — and a beautiful spot it is when the English Channel sparkles in the sunshine.

Remember Lord Mauleverer's yacht out there in the bay, shimmering in the early sunlight?

There was a time when the local residents agitated for a change of name, for they felt that Percy Avenue lacked dignity. However, the name survives to this day and visitors to Kent using the open-topped summer bus will still find it on the timetable as a regular halt.

Nothing could please Frank Richards more than this environment, for he loved the country, he loved the sea, and most of all he loved the solitary life. Though it was most unfortunate that shortly after taking up residence at 'Rose Lawn' he suffered a bad accident to his eyes, never all that strong, and although his work went from strength to strength a little of life's beauty was dimmed.

By now his workload and need for concentration was such that he did very little travelling save for the occasional trips to the Amalgamated Press. It would seem that by now he had settled down. In 1931, his old housekeeper retired and so Edith Hood, now a rosy cheeked young woman, become his housekeeper. He still continued to use 'Apple Trees' as a sort of second home when the fancy took him, but around 1938 the steep ascent proved too much for him and thereafter he used it so little that after the war he sold it.

The new owners renamed it 'Peacehaven', but it has since

reverted to its original name.

Though 'Rose Lawn' suited Frank Richards very well indeed, and helped give him the inspiration he sought, he found house guests could be distracting. It did not help things to have his flow of work interrupted or in any way disturbed, for his schedule was a demanding one, and these days deadlines simply had to be met.

A couple of years later he solved this problem by buying a bungalow opposite. This speculation served him well, for he could now accommodate his friends and relatives in comfort and, at the same time, be left in full possession of his privacy.

Basically, it was privacy he desired, for 'Rose Lawn' itself was adequately provided with rooms and upstairs alone there were four. Frank confined himself to a small bedroom with only the necessary furnishings, but also upstairs was his den, where he could work undisturbed.

Entry to this room was absolutely barred to all save Miss Hood, and even this was a grudging concession for a quick clean and dust only.

In post-war years, long after *The Magnet* and *Gem* had ceased publication and when the pressure of supplying the Companion Papers had gone, several of his admirers were given opportunities to visit 'Rose Lawn' and enter that sacred domain.

A Remington typewriter stood on a low table by the window. It was a very low table indeed, and the machine was of an old-fashioned kind. In front of the table was an equally low stool, topped by a small cushion, a spartan arrangement, but obviously comfortable enough.

Next to the table, to the right, was a long wall covered with bookshelves and books in front of which was a desk bearing another old typewriter. On the opposite wall was a fireplace and nearby stood a gramophone of vintage variety and also a small armchair.

More bookshelves occupied the remaining wall, and these bore a mixed array of reference and travel books, dictionaries and the works of Latin scholars. Novels by Walpole, Wodehouse and Talbot Baines Reed rubbed covers with the complete set of post-war Bunter books.

It was most interesting to glance quickly through some of the travel books and see many passages underlined. Obviously, Frank Richards had studied them a great deal in search of authentic background material for his famous *Magnet* overseas travel series. He had never visited India, Africa, Brazil, China, Egypt, nor the South Seas, and yet the series set in these places are regarded as some of his finest.

A short list of these travel books, which were later obtained and perused at leisure in the British Museum Reading Room, brought some fascinating discoveries. The descriptive detail in *China, The Land and People*, by Leonard Halford Buxton, had obviously been used a great deal in the China series of 1930, whilst Rider Haggard's theme in *Red Macaw* was used in the Brazil Series of 1936 together with Robert Peter Fleming's *Brazilian Adventure*.

No doubt the source material for the famed India series included *Our Eastern Empire — Stories of India* by Mrs E. Burrows, 1856. It is the belief of the publisher that a rich background source for the well-remembered Egypt series, 1932, was *Bella Donna* by Robert Hichens, originally published by William Heinemann in 1909 and, coincidentally, published again by Howard Baker Limited in 1969.

It may be noted that the name Baroudi featured largely in *Bella Donna* and was also featured in the Richards' Egypt series, published by Howard Baker in 1969 under the title *Land of the Pyramids*.

Many of the books on Frank Richards' shelves were late editions, and it was interesting to note that whilst our author's copy of *Pacific Tales* was dated 1925 the book had first appeared as far back as 1897. The author, George Louis Becke, was then writing about the South Seas in what was almost the time of the pirates and 'blackbirders'. It is consequently not to be wondered at that Frank Richards' sense of period in the Ken King stories, set in the Pacific, was many years out of date.

Also in the den was a cupboard where some of Frank Richards' own copies of his stories were stored. Unfortunately these showed no sign of ever having been treasured, and were tattered and tatty in the extreme. Many had covers missing, some had pages torn out — for use as pipe-lighters, perhaps? — and the only attempt to place them in any kind of chronological order had been to tie them up in rough bundles with string.

These bundles contained such successful series as The China series, Hollywood, Ravenspur Grange, Lancaster, Cavendale Abbey series, and many more. This was the residue of a much larger collection for, during the Second World War, Frank Richards disposed of many hundreds of *Magnets* and *Gems* as so much waste paper to salvage drives.

Downstairs, the lounge at the front of the house had a large window at one end which threw its light across a desk, and this end of the room was also furnished with a piano and a gramophone, to cater to our author's musical tastes. At the other end of the room were easy chairs and a settee close to the fireplace with its tobacco jar always in readiness.

Also handy was a metal ashtray which Frank Richards would hammer like a gong whenever he required Miss Hood's services. He had other methods of summoning assistance, too, such as banging on the coal scuttle with a poker, which certainly had the desired effect but which could be nerve racking to any visitor.

Illumination was poorer at this end of the room, daylight entering through three portholed windows, but a number of reading lamps gave the author the light that he needed for his failing eyesight.

Situated at the back of the house was the dining room, and its french windows led out to a neat and pleasant garden. For recreation, Frank Richards read a large old family Bible regularly and was also fond of French literature — though he confessed that he could not make sense of some of the modern French writers.

When not writing or reading or listening to music he loved to potter in his garden, not strenuously nor with any great skill, as Mr Mimble, but he would busy himself planting bulbs and lighting bonfires and doing other jobs of this nature.

For years he regularly rode a bicycle, for he was not a car driver. If he had to use a car — and he was given to travelling between Kingsgate and Hawkinge on the spur of the moment

— he would hire one, with someone else at the wheel. He was no driver. With a bicycle it was different, though it shouldn't have been, for with the increasing traffic in an ever-busier world he was fast becoming confused with what was going on around him.

A story has been related of the time he returned to Hampstead Garden Suburb and proceeded to plough his way on his cycle across the busy streets into the very heart of the traffic — until in the end he had to be rescued by a young policeman.

Probably the constable thought the old gentleman somewhat eccentric, whilst Frank Richards probably thought he was dealing with an officious young upstart. At all events, it was about this time that he gave up using his cycle, and it could well be that we owe it to this fact that stories continued to flow from his fertile brain. If continued, his cycling activities could have terminated his output once and for all.

Frank Richards' pleasures in life included tobacco, and great quantities of tobacco at that. Miss Hood used to keep him stocked up with at least a pound a week. He had progressed from cigars and cigarettes to being a great pipe-smoker, but alcohol interested him hardly at all.

Chess problems he appreciated, and he was a keen music lover. Mozart and opera, both serious and Gilbert and Sullivan, figured large in his record collection.

Some years after the end of the Second World War it was a delight to Frank Richards to offer hospitality to Thomas Arnold Johnson, who had just completed his composition of *The Greyfriars Suite* for piano solo. The swish of Quelch's cane, the Bunter cackle, Lord Mauleverer's yawn, the Bounder's swagger and defiance, and Alonzo Todd's meanderings were all portrayed in the music and brought a smile and sometimes a hearty laugh from Richards, and filled him with keen appreciation that his brain children should be so perpetuated.

In his early days, of course, our author had himself aspirations to be a popular song writer when, apart from *On the Ball*, his other compositions had included *Tell Me What is*

Love (introduced in the Greyfriars stories), *Come and Kiss Me, Honey, The Hand of the Far Away,* and *What's the Matter with England.*

For all of these songs Frank Richards wrote the lyrics whilst the music was composed by his brother-in-law, Percy Harrison.

Frank Richards was also a great cat-lover, and amongst his feline friends there was the handsome puss Lady Jane, and of course Sammy, who was pictured with Frank Richards on the cover of his Autobiography.

Magnet readers will no doubt recall the cat belonging to Mrs Kebble, the Greyfriars House-Dame/Matron which was the source of much amusement in many stories. A large black Tom named Thomas, he was blamed by Bunter every time a pie went missing from the pantry, and many times poor Thomas was thought to have been the main ingredient in one of Wun Lung's stews.

A dear old lady in the thirties used to regularly send small parcels of chopped liver and mincemeat to the *Magnet* office for the Greyfriars cat, but it is doubtful if Sammy or Lady Jane ever saw any of this.

Everything about Frank Richards' home and its surroundings was an aid to his work. The nearby Friends' House was probably the original locale of the 1935 Portercliffe Hall, *Magnet* series, or of the Eastcliffe Lodge series of 1940, and other nearby locations were written into other stories.

At the end of Percy Avenue the cliff, with a stretch of beach fifty feet below, has a flight of steps cut out of the rock leading downwards. This is very reminiscent of Pegg Bay. And who can fail to remember the marvellously funny incidents which befell Bunter riding a donkey on Margate beach?

Not too distant along the coast, and similar in setting, is Pegwell Bay, and a combination of these localities is likely to have been the real-life origin of the famous Greyfriars district.

Other familiar-sounding place-names near to 'Rose Lawn' excite the researcher. Close at hand there is Highcliffe and a hostelry by the name of *Captain Digby*. Only a short distance away is a Laurel Villa. Everything about the vicinity is redolent with the aroma of Greyfriars.

It can truly be said that those of us who love the stories of Frank Richards owe a lot to the atmosphere that was to surround him. Without it, the saga might have flickered away into nothing soon after the mediocre World War One period.

CHAPTER FOURTEEN

faraway places

The Famous Five of the Greyfriars Remove stood on the deck of the brig Mindanao, many a long thousand of miles from Greyfriars School.

A tropical sun burned their faces. The blue Pacific rolled around them. Ahead of the brig lay the island of Kalua-alua-lalua.

The lagoon, of deepest blue, lapped a beach of dazzling white, backed by tropical vegetation, the greenest of green.

Slanting palms, innumerable, nodded in the wind. The blossoms of the hibiscus glowed in patches of scarlet.

On the barrier reef the Pacific rollers broke in lines of endless foam, gleaming in the sunshine. Across the coral reef the Greyfriars juniors could see the lagoon within, and the island — spread like a gorgeous picture before their eyes.

Still in the late twenties, the breach remained between Frank Richards and Hedley O'Mant. But the fact that Frank Richards was determined to stay clear of the *Gem* as long as O'Mant was in charge did give him a little more time on his hands.

JOY HARINGTON, *who produces 'Billy Bunter of Greyfriars School' which begins on Tuesday, discusses the reasons for the world-wide popularity of*

The Owl of the Remove

'DID you ever read the *Magnet*?' Ask this question at almost any gathering and the response is electric. Sophisticated stock-brokers, dignified doctors, clergymen, actors, butchers, bakers and newspaper reporters grow visibly younger and talk each other down while pouring out reminiscences.

There are Greyfriars Clubs and Bunter Clubs; the stories have been translated into nearly every language and are available in Braille. What is the reason for their extraordinary and lasting appeal? For the answer we must turn to the author—Frank Richards. He started writing about Greyfriars schoolboys forty-two years ago, and is still writing about them today with the same spirit and vigour. Nothing has changed. Harry Wharton, Bob Cherry, Frank Nugent, Johnny Bull, and Hurree Jamset Ram Singh are still the Famous Five. Skinner, Scott, and Snoop are just as sneaky, Vernon Smith as bounderish; Mr. Quelch's gimlet eye still bores into the unfortunate juniors and Billy Bunter is still expecting a postal order.

In Bunter, Frank Richards has created a really first-rate character. There have been other fat boys in literature, but Bunter is the one who has become a household word. It is said that he was based on four different persons including an unnamed Victorian statesman and one can imagine the eager delight with which the author blended their characteristics and gave life to William George Bunter, the Owl of the Remove.

A family was invented for him: sister Bessie, young brother Sammy of the second form, and I remember in one story (it must have been twenty-five years ago) a cousin Wally who came to Greyfriars as a master and, though singularly like the fat porpoise in appearance, turned out to be such a sport.

As with Bunter, so with all the characters. Family, background, habits, expressions, and appearances have been painstakingly developed to satisfy a boy's appetite for detail, humour and adventure. This, I think, is the reason that the words *Magnet*, 'Greyfriars,' or 'Billy Bunter' will still start a conversational ball rolling quickly enough to delight any hostess.

A word to the uninitiated. You are possibly rather exasperated by the fanfare of welcome there has been and wonder what to expect. Don't expect a sophisticated comedy programme, a take-off of school life, a burlesque, or a 'period piece.' We are not presenting you with adult drama, but with schoolboy stories written for boys by one who, although now eighty years old, has a boy's heart.

Those who know the stories will watch, I hope, with a chuckle and a stirring of nostalgia. Those of you who are meeting Bunter and his chums for the first time will, I hope, get from your television sets on Tuesday evenings something of the delight that reading the latest adventure in the *Magnet* gave to us twelve, twenty, or forty-two years ago.

Bob Cherry

Mauleverer

Harry Wharton

Hurree Singh

Horace Coker

Johnny Bull

CHARACTERS AND CREATOR
Our centre-piece is a recent photograph of Frank Richards with his cat Sammy

Working at 80

HELPLESS old people ought to be cared for. That is the first duty of the young, who owe everything to them. But let young people get rid of the idea that all old persons are doddering old Dismal Jimmies who require philanthropic attention.

Mrs. Legge tells us in her article that she is "determined to find out what is happening to the old people."

I can tell her what is happening to one old person of 80 : he is carrying on his job, paying his way, in his leisure making a special study of Horace, and in lighter moments amusing himself by translating familiar old songs into Latin. That happy octogenarian is myself.

Frank Richards.
Rose Lawn, Kingsgate-on-Sea, Broadstairs, Kent.

▲ *Mr. Frank Richards is the author of the Greyfriars School stories in which Billy Bunter figures so prominently. Another series of these stories is to be televised shortly.*

Author Richards.

Joy Harington, producer of the series, shows Gerald Campion the look which she wants to see on the Bunter face in a particular scene

*Billy Bunter (Gerald Campion)
sneaks some of Bob Cherry's jam.*

Mr. Quelch (Kynaston Reeves) keeps an eye on his class. Here you see Billy Bunter played by (Gerald Campion)
Bob Cherry (Keith Faulkner), Johnny Bull (Barry Macgregor), and other members of the cast hard at work.

Below: Mr. Quelch, played by Raf de la Torre, is on the warpath. Billy's got the right answers—it's the questions that are wrong

Traditional caption to this would read: "Ouch! Leggo, you rotters!" howled Bunter as the Chums of the Remove deposited his fat form in the armchair

Rookwood had gone, and Greyfriars was his principal preoccupation. But there was in fact sufficient room in his schedules to enable him to exercise his creative genius once more — this time in the pages of *The Popular*.

Since its inauguration, *The Popular* had been most useful to the Companion Papers' office as a means of supplying the juvenile market with 'further' adventures of our author's creations. These were all old stories, of course, edited and revamped by *The Popular* editor, Arthur Aldcroft, to suit the paper's format.

Frank Richards was receiving a regular honorarium in acknowledgement of this re-use of old material and was therefore not disturbed by the arrangement.

But then, on January 21st 1928, came a series of stories unprecedented in *Popular* history for they were all new originals — Westerns written by our author under the guise of 'Ralph Redway'.

Whilst it is true that Frank Richards' main contribution to memorable juvenile literature was through the school story it is also a fact that he had written notable tales in other categories, including adventures set in the Wild West.

But nothing that had gone before equalled these new offerings.

The *Popular* Westerns introduced a new hero, 'The Rio Kid', and were purely boys' stories, delightfully written in a style exclusive to themselves.

At first The Rio Kid would appear to have been nameless, and though later he called himself Kid Carfax one cannot be sure that this was his true name, for there is a slight air of mystery about him. As to his age, he was probably in his late teens, and he was certainly an outlaw. The story of his downfall is an unfortuante one.

On his way back to the Double Bar Ranch from the Bank in Frio, the Kid was robbed of the ranch payroll, but, as he was well known to be quick on the draw, it was not surprising that Rancher Dawney found his story difficult to believe. Unmercifully, he ran the Kid off the ranch, branding him a thief.

Frank Richards had used the theme of wrongful accusation

a hundred times previously in his school tales, and he skilfully rang the changes on it to suit the boy from the Rio Grande. Subsequently, Dawney offered a reward of a thousand dollars for the Kid's capture, and he was now an outlaw with further charges being levelled against him all of the time.

Ironically enough, when eventually the Kid was able to convince Dawney of his innocence of the original payroll robbery it was too late to make any difference: he had been branded.

During the three years that the Rio Kid rode the range in the *Popular*, until the autumn of 1930, every story could be said to be of the highest quality, a supreme effort on the part of the author. But the stories still lacked that certain indefinable something which would have immortalised them.

Seven years later, the flagging circulation of the *Modern Boy* prompted the editors to see what the return of the Rio Kid could do for the situation. These stories were not of the same high quality as the original series, and some doubts were voiced at the time as to whether they came from the same pen. Certainly they did nothing for the fortunes of the *Modern Boy*.

Amalgamated Press records confirm that Frank Richards did write them all, despite their poor quality. Indeed, he was in the habit of sending them up to Fleetway House in batches of six at a time. The Rio Kid made his last bow in the *Magnet* Texas series of 1938 in the company of the boys of Greyfriars — a brilliant but much neglected character.

A little over a year after the first appearance of the Rio Kid in the *Popular*, C.M. Down had launched a new paper, *Modern Boy*, and put Charles Boff in charge of it. Frank Richards was commissioned to write for it and the first issue appeared on February 11th 1928. It was described as 'The Most Up-to-date Boys' Paper'.

Though it had a fair run, it is hard to believe that it could ever have enjoyed a tremendous success. Perhaps it was ahead of its time in some respects, but in others it was dull, lacking sparkle and colour. However many virtues Frank Richards had as a writer it is doubtful whether even his most ardent admirers could suggest that his work was trendy. His slang and his type of slapstick humour was far removed from that of the youth of the inter-war years.

One concludes that C.M. Down commissioned Frank Richards to write for his new brain child well-knowing that his current commitments were restrictive to his abilities. It is also a fact that the name of Frank Richards was not, at this time, used as an attraction to launch a best-seller.

With the debut of his new character Ken King, Frank Richards reverted to his real name of Charles Hamilton almost to cloak his identity. An additional blurb to the by-line stated that the stories were written in collaboration with Sir Alan Cobham, then the holder of several world speed records and a household name. The inference was, of course, that Cobham's name would sell *Modern Boy*, but not the name of Frank Richards. Naturally, Cobham got a fat cheque for doing nothing but lend his name to a few stories whilst Frank Richards did all the donkey work.

Years later, when questioned on the matter, Frank Richards seemed unaware that Cobham's name was on the stories at all and, in any event, the collaboration plainly did not have any great effect upon sales because after a few months Cobham's name was dropped from the by-line.

King of the Islands, the boy skipper of the trading ketch 'The Dawn', was the last of the author's really great creations. Ken King was supposedly about seventeen or eighteen — a remarkable fact considering his ability to handle the many tense and hazardous adventures he experienced. Anyone twice his age would have been proud to possess King's skill and strength of character in dealing with the rogues who crossed his path. The fact that many of his foes actually feared him makes his prowess even more incredible.

Richards' genius in this series is demonstrated in the fact that even though the background was of a monotonous sameness — the restricted tropical beaches, coral islands, and uncharted seas of the Pacific — he still managed by means of many twists in the plot to keep going for over two hundred stories.

To help him, he introduced pearlers, cannibals of the

traditional variety, and an abundance of treasure. Throughout the series Ken King shared his adventures with his Australian mate, Kit Hudson, and Koko, the Kanaka boy.

Again one is forced to admit that in the South Seas series we had a situation akin to that in the Rio Kid tales: the manners, customs, and even the quaint pidgin English of some of the characters belonged to an earlier period than that in which they were supposedly set. When, at a later date, Ken King met the Famous Five in the Second Pacific series of 1938 one could sense the vast difference in time between the two sets of characters. However, Frank Richards told a story so cleverly that one's eyes slid over these lapses from reality, and readers simply made a mental note that on their next trip to the South Seas they must steer clear of the cannibals of Melanesia.

By 1930 the value of the *Popular* was reaching its end so far as our author's reprints were concerned: the store of St. Jim's and Rookwood stories was virtually all used up, though there was still some material available from the Greyfriars files. Now the continuing one-sided feud between Frank Richards and Hedley O'Mant which had already cost *Gem* readers dear began to injure the *Popular* and also to bite deep into our author's own earnings in no uncertain way.

To meet the obvious lack of original material, he had produced his series 'Popolaki Patrol' appearing under the name of Charles Hamilton. Set in the Congo it had a three month run between two series of Rio Kid stories. Probably the least read of all his creations they again were exciting, well-written stories dealing with mysterious black tribes, man-eating lions, and situations reminiscent of the Tarzan tales. But being limited in scope they failed to enjoy any considerable success.

Another character created in 1930 was Bunny Hare, who also appeared in *Modern Boy*, in a series of twelve. This little known series said much for Frank Richards' geographical knowledge, for though it commenced at his beloved sunny Margate it continued through France, Gibraltar, Morocco and Tunis, finally ending in the ruins of Carthage.

Altogether his vivid descriptions of 'faraway places' say a

great deal for the fertile imagination and inventive genius of an author who in his lifetime never put a foot outside the confines of Western Europe.

CHAPTER FIFTEEN

other schools, Will Hay, and Bendover

It was the end of an era when, in 1931, the axe came down on the *Popular* and the editor, Arthur Aldcroft, moved over to *The Gem* to handle the preparation of St. Jim's stories for reprint publication.

Hedley O'Mant was chosen to edit the successor to the *Popular*: a new paper to be known as *The Ranger*.

This brand new modern style of paper suited O'Mant completely, nor did he really mind that Frank Richards would be writing a brand new series of school stories for it. This arrangement had been made strictly between Monty Haydon and Frank Richards, and the stories began to appear in 1932.

In keeping with the new look of *The Ranger* Grimsdale was a school situated on the borders of Yorkshire and Lancashire and was in essence bright and exciting. The school was set in the north of England in an attempt to win back some of the vast number of readers who lived there and had earlier deserted Amalgamated Press papers for those of D.C. Thomson.

Jim Dainty was the hero of the series, and like Harry Wharton was the unwilling new boy, rebellious and spoilt by his mother during his father's prolonged absence, and sent to his father's old school. An immensely readable and likeable series it had, unfortunately, too brief a career to allow for the progressive creation of a convincing atmosphere. Needless to say, Frank Richards had another opportunity to play around with his characters' names, and his tools were the two boys Bacon and Bean. He also had a rather objectionable fat boy named Von Splitz, but he had none of Bunter's dubious charm.

In 1934 he created the short-lived but very well-known 'School for Slackers' for *Modern Boy*. A fine set of seventeen stories with a fascinating if a little improbable theme, Frank Richards always claimed these to be his most polished creations. High Coombe was a picturesque old building in Devonshire, an ancient rambling pile, where James McCann, M.A., one-time cricket captain of Loamshire, strove to permanently cure a hopeless crowd of slacking schoolboys. Of course, his task was never satisfactorily accomplished and thus each story left the way clear for another.

In 1935, R.C. Hewitt took over Aldcroft's chair at *The Gem*, and Frank Richards started to write a new series of stories for that paper. He made it another Wild West series, 'The Packsaddle Bunch'. These school stories were set in Santana County in the Lone Star State of Texas, near to Squaw Mountain on the banks of the Rio Frio and were full of action and excitement. The fact that no girl ever made an appearance in the stories leaves one with the assumption that the risks were too great. Though an enjoyable series, 'The Packsaddle Bunch' lacked the dignity of the former Cedar Creek stories and a more improbable school it would be hard to find.

Bill Sampson, the headmaster, was one of the fastest men on the draw in Texas, but his scholastic ability was almost nil. His main asset was brawn, and he ruled the cow town with a rod of iron.

The leading schoolboy character in the series was Dick Carr, an English boy who had gone out to Texas to join his father, manager of the store in the town of Hard Tack. The stories cluttered with typical Richards' Western-style villains, and school life was something of a riot. Not by any means the most outstanding of the author's creations, the series was written in a vein typical of the new-look publications. This time Frank Richards seemed to have gone a long way to update his style.

Continuing his association with *Modern Boy*, in the same year he created a new series featuring Len Lex, the schoolboy detective of Oakshott School, a typical series of Richards' mystery stories with no pretensions of originality.

Len Lex, nephew of Chief Inspector Nixon of Scotland Yard, is sent to Oakshott in the guise of a normal schoolboy to search for a crook known as 'The Sussex Man'. Plenty of mystery and detection ensues, but there is also a fair share of the frolics and japes of regular school life, and Len Lex is not too staid to enjoy it.

In the end, Len Lex fades unobtrusively out of the stories, having successfully withheld his true purpose from his schoolmates. In making Len Lex a Fifth Former, and not a junior, the author gave the series a great deal more plausibility, and in 'The Sussex Man' series he made his mixture of suspense and mystery much more gripping than usual. It cannot be denied that his greatest fault in anything verging on a mystery story was that no matter how obvious was the villain of the piece the only one who seemed to have the story sewn up was the reader himself.

Percy Montague Haydon, known to everyone as 'Monty' or 'P.M.', was the controlling editor of a large group of boys' papers. He was far senior to C.M. Down — though not in years — and had worked his way up from the position of office boy.

He was a creative genius, shrewd, full of enthusiasm, and the perfect man for the job. During the First World War he had served with great distinction as an officer, winning the M.C. If Monty had not chosen boys' papers as his career he could easily have been a diplomat, for he was an expert at making things run smoothly and in patching up differences between editors, managing editors and authors.

Not all of Monty's ideas reaped the success that he hoped, but his maxim was that unless one tried out new experiments and put new ideas to the test one could not look for success at all. And some of his ideas had been as advanced as their success had been staggering. One idea, for example, had been to print a seven and sixpenny novel by a top-class author in his paper *The Thriller*, and sell it for only twopence! Now he wanted a series of slapstick school stories featuring the very popular comedian of the time, the great Will Hay[1].

This splendid comic had had great success on the stage with hilarious comedy sketches in which he portrayed a seedy, shifty and incompetent schoolmaster. Now he had gone into films, and the first two were outstanding current successes — box office hits.

"Several writers have written pilot stories," Haydon told Frank Richards, "but all of them are not quite what I wanted. You are the only man to write them in a way to make the readers lap them up."

Frank Richards must have felt flattered. The series was to run in the new paper, *The Pilot* which had succeeded *The Ranger*.

Walter Shute had actually written six stories featuring Will Hay, but these were indefinitely shelved as not being funny enough. Edwy Searles Brooks, writer of the St Franks series in *The Nelson Lee Library* had also written a few, and in his case some were used later.

Diplomatically, Monty Haydon had smoothed over the Richards/O'Mant spot of bother quite easily. He had simply told Frank Richards always to see him personally on his visits to Fleetway House, and that he would always deal with his work. The two men got on very well.

Monty was a small boy when Frank Richards had created Ferrers Locke, the detective, but with his shrewd eyes, clear-cut features and his youthful zest he must have reminded our author of his creation instantly.

1 Before the First World War the comic *Funny Wonder* had started a comic strip featuring Charlie Chaplin, and drawn by Bert Brown. Strips featuring other famous comedians had followed, including Laurel and Hardy in *Film Fun*, who were drawn by G.W. Wakefield, who had also drawn the later Rookwood illustrations. The use of these stars, all household names, had boosted the comics' circulations considerably.

Progressing from this, Monty Haydon had thought of having famous stars in the realms of sport, stage and screen relate their early lives in story form, and it was just one short step onward to reach slapstick school stories featuring Will Hay.

Haydon, it should also be said, was a very clever investor, and quite freely gave useful tips on shares in the City. Unlike Mr Samuel Bunter who played Bulls and Bears with no great success, Monty's tips were, more often than not, highly lucrative.

Many years later Frank Richards was able to make a good deal of money on some Gainsborough Pictures shares as a result of a tip from Monty Haydon, and also to reap a rich harvest from some Mexican Mining shares into the bargain.

Curiously, in his autobiography, Frank Richards mentions the Will Hay series, but gives the wrong paper:

> 'There was another series I remember with pleasure, which featured the popular Will Hay. This series was published in a paper called The Ranger, edited by Montague Haydon . . .The Will Hay series lasted for a long time, and it is a pleasant episode in Frank's memory.'

Dates, as he freely admitted, were never Frank Richards' strong point, as the *Pilot* had been running for almost eighteen months before the Will Hay stories commenced.

Perhaps he was under the impression that *The Ranger* had never changed its name.

Characteristic of Frank Richards' favourite theme for the arrival of a newcomer to a school, Will Hay arrived at Doddlebury Station for Bendover School in *The Pilot* No.72 February 13th 1937.

All the boys of the Fourth were lined up on the platform to meet him, and what a colourful crowd they were. And with what a rich assortment of names.

Headmaster was Dr. Erasmus Shrubb, a kindly man modelled on the lines of Dr. Locke. Master of the Fifth was a Mr Choot: a portly, pompous individual who had hunting trophies in his study and was almost a double of Mr Prout. French Master was a Monsieur Le Bon — nicknamed Mosso Bong — and another Master, fond of the bottle, was called Mr Shandy. The nearest pub to the school had a familiar ring about it. It was named 'The Three Fishers'.

Boys of the Fourth, of which Will Hay was master, included a Dicky Bird, the Captain; Issy Cumming, the Jewish Junior; and the two cads and black sheep, Reggie Pyke and Fruity Snell. Will Hay was, of course, ragged unmercifully in his early days at Bendover but, as in his films, he always managed to hold his own by sheer cunning and great wit. Although a buffoon in appearance, he was shrewd, and in time became very popular with the boys of his form.

Series themes included a Yankee Trader from the South Seas and a crooked master trying to get the job of Headmaster, while single stories featured ventriloquism and other well-known *Magnet* devices. One such theme was identical with an early *Magnet* when, in answer to a bogus advertisement, a number of ladies came to the school to offer themselves as Will Hay's marriage partner, when what he actually wanted was a new bike!

Possibly due to a commitment to write new stories for *The Modern Boy* as well as *The Magnet* each week, Frank Richards began to lose interest in Will Hay stories and they first became shorter with the introduction of a Will Hay comic strip, and then ceased altogether with issue No. 129 of March 19th 1938.

The stories were not the success that everyone had hoped for, nor, curiously, was the Will Hay comic strip in *Jolly Comic*. It is difficult to say why, for Will Hay himself went from strength to strength with Moore Marriot as Harbottle and Graham Moffat as the impertinent fat boy in later films.

Meantime, in these busy days, little did Frank Richards know that in less than two short years he would sustain the biggest blow of his entire writing career, and he would be busy no more.

CHAPTER SIXTEEN

morals and mores

What influence Frank Richards had on many young lives is a question that is asked many times, and the answer must surely be one of two things. Either he was a good moral influence or no influence at all, for it seems impossible that he could have been a bad one.

Though strict disciplinarians may insist that to tell stories of boys who gambled and smoked, even though they were eventually found out and punished, was sufficient encouragement for some boys to do likewise, few people will take this line of reasoning seriously.

Television, films and horror comics have all been blamed unmercifully for depraving the young. But can anyone truly compare *The Magnet* or *Gem* with a horror comic?

Even so, some years ago one lone librarian at Ipswich put her foot down. Cassell's Bunter books were all taken off open shelves and only supplied on demand. The rest of the time they were hidden behind a curtain side-by-side with other 'dubious' literature.

The librarian explained that she felt the Bunter stories were a bad influence on children and the style and humour not for the modern child. Billy Bunter and his fat sister Bessie were gluttons, and inclined children to poke fun at fat people.

This was a foolish act that was soon rectified for, far from being corrupting, Frank Richards operated his characters on a high moral plane. The good prevailed over the bad every time. Smoking was a dirty habit that should be discouraged from the beginning. Gambling frequently led to deceit and sometimes resulted in a criminal act. Drinking, of course, was downright unhealthy.

One must remember that Frank Richards was two or three generations back in attitude, not merely one. Morally he was a Victorian. When he started to write it was accepted that stories for the young should always be didactic in moral tone, that they should teach and show good triumphing over evil. The principle of setting a high moral code in stories for boys seemed to Victorians a duty.

Some people would call Frank Richards a hypocrite for writing in this fashion when he himself smoked and gambled to a great extent. But, because of this, was he obliged to write stories praising gamblers? In this case Frank Richards differentiated between himself, the writer, and Charles Hamilton, the private citizen. In his world they were different people, and the first had a duty to his readers.

There was no doubt that Frank Richards was a deeply religious man, and he carried this faith with him throughout his life. "Religion is a sacred subject," he used to say, and very rarely introduced it in his stories.

Callers without an appointment were turned away from Rose Lawn for the logical reason that if he saw one he should see them all, and this would leave him little time for writing new stories. However, clergymen were always welcome as flowers in May and he really enjoyed their conversation. Incidentally, many readers of *The Magnet* must have failed to note that Dr Herbert H. Locke was actually a clergyman, being a Doctor of Divinity.

Around 1948 Frank Richards wrote a little book on religion entitled *Faith and Hope*, but this was fated never to be published. He often lamented this fact, and complained that all the publishers wanted was Bunter. He went on to describe the book:

"It is the humble attempt on the part of an old

man, now very nearly at the end, to strengthen Christian belief and faith in young minds in these doubting days. I shall hope at least to cause some to share my own belief. Those troubled by doubt would probably have their minds eased in the light of experience and reflection."

In the early days of the Great War the editor of *The Magnet*, H.A. Hinton, asked Frank Richards if he would write a special story with a religious theme. Curiously enough, in those days many schools still imposed a ban on *The Magnet* and *Gem* under the mistaken impression that the stories were of the penny dreadful type.

The author flatly refused Hinton's request on the grounds that he strongly believed religion and boys' fiction did not mix. Briefly, he never believed in forcing a sacred subject on to boys and girls.

George Richmond Samways, a sub-editor, was then instructed by Hinton to write the required story, and it appeared in *The Magnet* No.400 entitled *The Sunday Crusaders*. It was a rather Victorian and sentimental tale wherein Skinner eventually 'saw the light', but it would be very unfair to level the blame at the writer for its maudlin sentimentality, for he was only carrying out editorial instructions.

With the publication of the story in 1915, the young Samways proudly took a number of copies down to his old school and offered them to the Head, who was regarded as a pious and sanctimonious person, to prove that *The Magnet* did indeed sport a highly moral tone.

Samways' school had had a strict ban on the circulation of *The Magnet* and *Gem*, and it had meant dire punishment if a pupil were caught with one of 'those wretched books'. It is not recorded what impression Samways' crusading effort actually made on his erstwhile Headmaster, but one gathers that the prejudice remained for some time before the ban was eventually lifted.

Copies of this issue were sent to every clergyman listed in *Crockford's Directory*, and many answering tributes were received. These letters were subsequently published in the pages of *The Magnet*.

Whilst it is true that some readers may have been gained by this exercise, "it is equally possible," as another sub-editor remarked at that time, "that an equal number were lost, simply because boys do not like to have religion thrust down their throats."

Frank Richards' own contribution to the theme was usually confined to mention of boys going for a Sunday walk after 'divers' — Divine Service.

Another clear trait in Frank Richards' character was that at all times he was an out-and-out Englishman, as loyal to the British Crown as any man could ever be, and full of admiration for the British way of life. He belonged to that generation when the words 'gentlemen' and 'ladies' had a current meaning, and had not become almost exclusively used to denote separate sections of public conveniences.

There is no doubt that he thought foreigners funny, probably in the same way that the foreigner thinks the Englishman truly hilarious, with his strange little ways. In his stories Fisher T. Fish, the American, always obnoxiously after the almighty dollar, Wun Lung, the Chinese, complete with pig-tail and pidgin talk, and the excitable French Master nicknamed 'Mosso' were all presented in a stylised form as figures of fun.

Certainly he was far from being racist, as he made the Indian boy, Hurree Singh, with his remarkable flow of English, a member of The Famous Five to try and rid the youthful mind of colour prejudice. Boys were growing up in the great Empire and a few unfortunately still called coloured people 'black niggers' — including Bunter, of course, who was soon told the error of his ways.

Jews were also given very sympathetic treatment, and this is noteworthy, for they were still the object of vilification and abuse in England prior to the First World War. Monty Newland had a bad time on his arrival at Greyfriars at the hands of some of the Removites, including Bunter again with his cry of "Yah, Sheeny!"

Frank Richards tried to show what a good, clean, decent chap Monty Newland was, as a representative of the Hebrew race, but the story, according to a sub-editor of the time, brought adverse reaction from a vast number of readers in the East End of London.

Many, whilst appreciating the author's fine motives, thought that he had emphasised that there was a big difference between Jews and other boys. It would have been better if Monty Newland had been accepted as 'one of them' straight away. Curiously, Solly Lazarus of Courtfield was also a target for dislike and even more so his father, who often appeared in Greyfriars stories as a purveyor of costumes for amateur actors, William Wibley being easily his best customer.

Mr Lazarus simply had to be a pawnbroker, of course, and this seems to be an area in which Frank Richards' good motives rather misfired. He rather overdid things. The result was that he tended to play down the Jewish question in later stories.

The Magnet and *Gem* had been started when Lloyd George was in power, and the then strong Liberal Government had begun to 'soak the rich' — albeit very mildly — and preach the cause of 'making everybody somebody'.

Frank Richards poked fun at this, especially through the medium of Gussy in *The Gem*, who thought he would never sit in the House of Lords since long before he was able to do so it would have been abolished by the egalitarian Liberals.

One does get the impression that Frank Richards did not favour Lloyd George's ideals, and if this was so he must have thought Socialism an absolutely crackpot political idea. Consequently it was only to be expected that he would use the rather inane *Gem* character, Skimpole, as his vehicle to lampoon Socialism in a story devoted to Skimpole's new found craze.

Reading the story today, one can see it as farce from start to finish, for the central character has only the vaguest idea of the political ideals involved. All of Frank Richards' stories which touched on politics tended to be scratchy on detail. *Bunter the Bolshevik* is a case in point, and *Only Gussy's Way*, in which the author poked fun at nationalisation. In this latter story, the St. Jim's boys, who were

YAROOOH!

"I SAY, you fellows—"
"Buzz off, Bunter!"
"But listen—"
"Roll away, porpoise!"
"Look here, you rotters—"
"Oh, let's bump him, fellows!"
"Leggo you beasts! Ouch! Ow!
Yarooooooh!"
"Ha, ha, ha!"

The dialogue is familiar to millions. It has occurred in some form or other in practically every story of Greyfriars school—and it's nigh on fifty years since they were first published in the *Magnet.*

To men past middle age it recalls the days of their youth—the latest school story read furtively under the lid of the school desk; a whole string of characters who made up the boys of Greyfriars—Harry Wharton, Bob Cherry, Frank Nugent, Johnny Bull, Hurree Jamset Ram Singh, Skinner, Snoop and dozens of others. Not forgetting Mr. Quelch, the master of the Remove, whose chief line of attack seemed to be: "What is the meaning of this unseemly disturbance?"

Old-fashioned, out-dated? Not on your life! For the boys of Greyfriars, with Billy Bunter as the undoubted star, now appear in a regular series on Children's TV (Memo to dads: There's another one next Saturday). And the author of them is still the same man—Charles Hamilton, now over eighty, who as "Frank Richards" has written millions of words of school adventure. He will recall that in spite of the high moral tone of the stories, Skinner and Snoop, the Cads of the Remove, sometimes smoked a cigarette! So the stories were sometimes frowned upon by those in authority.

Over the years various attempts were made to film the Greyfriars characters, but they always failed when it came to Bunter. There was nobody, it seemed, who could be made to look exactly like the "fat porpoise" of the illustrations.

Joy Harington, producer of the series, had to face up to the same problems which had baffled the film people when she tried to find someone to play Bunter. If a boy were fat enough, then he was too young, or couldn't act, or found it difficult to get time off from school to attend rehearsals. Then she saw 33-year-old Gerald Campion, with his chubby expressive face. This, plus his enthusiasm for the part, told her that her search was over. For with the addition of costume, padding and make-up (not forgetting the pince-nez) Gerald should become the most convincing Fat Boy.

And how does it feel to be a present-day Bunter?

Yes, it's the anguished cry of Billy Bunter, fat schoolboy favourite of nearly half a century and now a top star of children's TV. Gerald Campion is every inch the Owl of the Remove

By JACQUELINE SHARMAN

"They never tire of him"

After spending the afternoon in studio E I can give you one answer—very hot! When I arrived, a tea break had just been called. Technicians and the young actors playing the boys of Greyfriars had rushed off to grab a bun and a drink. Billy Bunter the schoolboy would have been the first to go, but Billy Bunter of TV wanted no jam tarts, however scrumptious. All he wanted was a cigarette and a cold drink. And most of all, he wanted to sit down. So we went to his dressing room and he was able to talk about his other personality.

Why the desire to flop in a chair?

"Feel that," he demanded, and I rather gingerly prodded his stomach. "There are 22 lbs. of padding there, and it's no joke carrying it about in this weather! I haven't got the Bunter figure, or anything like it, so I have to be padded—well padded!"

But he liked his role.

"Bunter is a lot of fun to do, and I thoroughly enjoy the series. Bunter is as fresh as ever to the modern child. It's not my favourite part, mind you. He's a little too mean, with a nasty turn of humour. No, my particular joy is Toad of Toad Hall. Now there's a character. He may be naughty and conceited, but he has such charm. And that's what's lacking in Billy. But the children laugh at him and like him—and that's the main thing."

A knock at the door reminded us that it was time for another run-through in the studio. Gerald struggled to his feet, adjusted his padding, and we made our way back to Studio E.

Joy Harington was busy—this time worrying about the next production, which called for seven different settings to be put up in the studio. Could they be reduced? Somehow it would have to be done.

Meanwhile, back to the present, and some complicated camera work on a setting representing the Form Room where, in the Greyfriars tradition, something is always happening to interrupt the lessons.

But afterwards Joy confirmed the present-day popularity of the Owl of the Remove. "It seems that as each generation comes along they discover Bunter and continue to enjoy his adventures as they grow up. They never tire of him."

And Tony Arnold, studio manager, added: "After all, space ships are all very fine, but the schoolboy likes something he can associate himself with. And every boy can recognise something of himself in the boys of Greyfriars school."

So beware, all school teachers. Examine all chairs for drawing pins—and never open a door without checking that there is no bucket of water perched on top awaiting your entrance.

Frank Richards at work in his study.

Photo's: The Charles Hamilton Museum.

EDUCATION

Forever Bunter

Of all the public schoolboys in Britain —not even excluding Tom Brown—none is better known or more persistent than Billy Bunter of Greyfriars. A round, owlish fellow, he is forever stealing other chaps' "tuck" (cakes, cream puffs, tarts, toffee). He is hopeless at athletics, can't seem to spell ("I wood have toled you myself but you wood not lissen . . ."), is perpetually in a "digamma," and is constantly delivering such Bunterisms as "How sharper than a thankless child it is to have a toothless serpent."

Billy Bunter is always in trouble: he is "whopped" ("Wow! Oh! Oh, crumbs! Wow!"), smacked ("Yarooh! Ow! Wow! Ooogh! Beast! Wow!"), and "spifflicated" unmercifully ("Ow! I say—wow! I say—oh, crikey!"). But in spite of such misadventures, Billy Bunter has managed to survive—at the same age and in the same school—for 45 years. Last week Britons were once again reading all about him in a new book called *Billy Bunter's Brain-Wave*, by Charles Hamilton.

Mostly Richards. Over the years, Author Hamilton has turned out an estimated 70 million words about Bunter and others like him. A wispy, monkish little man of 82 who wears a black skull cap and translates Horace, he has used a number of pen names: Martin Clifford, creator of Tom Merry of St. Jim's; Hilda Richards, creator of Bessie Bunter; Ralph Redway for the Rio Kid; Peter Todd for Herlock Sholmes; and Owen Conquest for Jimmy Silver. But mostly, Charles Hamilton is Bunter's creator, Frank Richards. "To relatives and bankers and the inspector of taxes," says he, "I am still Charles Hamilton; to everybody else, including myself, [I am] Frank Richards."

Charles Hamilton first turned into Frank Richards in 1908, when at 37 he began publishing his Bunter stories in a halfpenny weekly called the *Magnet*. To his own astonishment, Bunter soon became a household word, and the entire British Empire seemed to take Greyfriars to its heart. It was a quiet, stiff-upper-lip sort of world where sex and politics were never mentioned, and no gentleman ever thought of tattling on another. Missionaries read about it in Malaya; traders took the *Magnet* along to Australia; soldiers snatched it up in their canteens in India. Eventually the time came when Charles Hamilton was forced to declare that Frank Richards had become a "public character." He wrote Richards' autobiography, even started a new school series with a younger Richards as the hero.

Fifty a Minute. According to the autobiography, Richards-Hamilton had "a tremendous memory. He learned the *Lay of the Last Minstrel* by heart before he was twelve." He could also recite huge chunks of Shakespeare, Goethe, Dante and Keats, could play the "immortal game" of chess in his head, learned to write at the rate of 50 words a minute. Not even his arrest

BILLY FACING THE HEADMASTER

. . . IN CORRIDOR COLLISION

R. J. Macdonald. © Charles Skilton Ltd.
. . . SPIFFLICATED BY SCHOOLMATE
"Wow! Oh! Oh, crumbs! Wow!"

in Austria as an enemy alien during World War I could keep him from his typewriter. "Military fatheads," declared Richards-Hamilton, "might come and go, but Billy Bunter went on forever."

Today Bunter's immortality seems assured. He is a constant topic of conversation at London's Old Boys' Book Club —a society of 400 greying authors, schoolmasters, actors and civil servants who collect juvenilia and have as their motto *Puer Manebit*. Billy Bunter is on TV and appears in a comic strip, and since 1947 the twelve volumes about him have sold 180,000 copies.

Toffees to Stickers. In spite of wars and depressions, he and his schoolmates go right on talking their 50-year-old slang (running is "cutting"; a bicycle is a "jigger"; spectacles are "gig lamps"; toffees are "stickers"; a cad is a "tick"; and whopping lies are "crammers"). In 45 years not one of them has grown a day older or changed one jot. Quelch is still the stern master of the remove or lower fourth form; "Mossoo" Charpentier is still the excitable French teacher; young Loder is still the rotter of the sixth. The captain of the school is still "Good Old Wingate," who always manages to kick the winning goal ("Ain't he a nut? Ain't he a prize-packet? Ain't he the jolly old goods, and then some? Ain't he a Briton? Good old Wingate!").

In his neat, little Kent cottage, where he lives with an aging cat, Charles Hamilton-Frank Richards allows no criticism of either Billy Bunter or Greyfriars. Once when the late George Orwell, in a solemn essay, accused Richards of being snobbish, Hamilton snapped back: "It is an actual fact that, in this country at least, noblemen generally are better fellows than commoners." To the criticism that he makes all his foreigners "funny," he replied: "I must shock Mr. Orwell by telling him that foreigners *are* funny." Once a friend asked him: "Don't you ever think of doing anything better?" Stroking his cat and blinking myopically, Charles Hamilton gave a typical Frank Richards reply. "No," said he, "you see, there *isn't* anything better."

The Quest

As an example of how far Americans will go in their quest for culture, nothing beats the Great Books tour through Europe. Sponsored by St. John's College of Annapolis, Md., it has swept its 22 travelers (including four teachers, one college dean, one school principal, three students, one librarian and assorted secretaries and housewives) through five countries, a dozen Great Books, and innumerable castles, cathedrals and birthplaces.

The idea of the tour was to read and discuss the books right on their authors' old stamping grounds—or as close to the grounds as possible. By last week everyone was feeling a trifle numb. "It's been very interesting, of course," said one traveler. "Like when we were in Florence we studied Dante and somebody else. I forget exactly who."

caravanning at the time, arrived at a small town in the middle of a by-election. Skimpole's Uncle Chinn was the candidate for The Red Flag, and on being handed a leaflet urging *Vote for Chinn! Chinn Stands for Nationalisation!* Monty Lowther took out a pencil and added a few comments of his own. *'There are only a million officials in the country at present. Nationalise, and have a million more!'*

Anything as far to the left as Communism would, one imagines, have verged on The Black Hand Gang as far as Frank's views were concerned. Shades of mysterious Russians in cloaks with bombs at the ready! But it must be said that politics played a very small part in the story scene at Greyfriars and St. Jim's. And it is also true that Frank Richards was impartially happy to deride all politicians. They were all figures of fun to him.

It is no secret that Frank Richards could find little compassion in his heart for Income Tax officials, or indeed for any member of the Ministries which indicated the sums to be levied upon one's hard earned income.[1] He voiced his opinions through the mouth of Mr Samuel Bunter with whom distaste for the enforced payment of income tax amounted to an obsession on which he never ceased to carp — especially when his first born son, William George, tried to extract a remittance from him.

Frank Richards' objections to tax-paying were certainly not politically motivated, for in this regard it mattered little to him who the Government of the day was. They all levied taxes.

In political persuasion he was probably mildly right wing, though George Orwell, in his attack upon him, suggested he was a diehard Tory.

His own writings suggest that he was by nature both a humane and liberal man with a love of conservative virtues.

He felt that the world should not be made over to layabouts; that it was up to the individual to make and pay

1 At the outbreak of the Second World War, Frank Richards was placed in the awkward position of having a large tax demand with no income to pay it. In 1940 he sent his surtax demand to the Amalgamated Press and suggested that the company ought to pay it for him, since it had placed him in that predicament. H.J. Garrish, who handled the business in Monty Haydon's absence on war-work, was equally vitriolic in his reply.

his own way. It was not for the State to support the slacker, and at the same time the servant was not necessarily as good as his master.

All of this said, there was room for charity in the world, and concern for the worse off. But good works should be done privately, not by the State.

His personal feelings on the class question tended to show in his stories, and on more than one occasion gave rise to the question: Was Frank Richards a snob?

It is doubtful if he was, consciously or intentionally. But it is quite obvious that his knowledge of working class life was very limited indeed.

Just as what went on at St. Jim's and Greyfriars bore little relation to real life at English Public Schools, so Frank Richards' portrayal of working class speech is inaccurate and condescending.

This could not be better illustrated than in a scene at the school gates of Rookwood where a working class character addresses Cecil Cuthbert Montmorency, ex-boot-boy, but now a member of the aristocracy.

"George! Hi, George! Don't you know your old pal 'Orace what used to clean the boots at the 'all where you was in buttons?" Mack, the porter, and therefore another figure of fun, says, "Who's he torkin to? There ain't nobody 'ere named 'Uggins. You silly owl that's Master Montmorency!" "Wot!" said Horace Lurchey. "Montmorency!" said Mack crushingly, "now clear hoff."

At the same time, Frank Richards would also poke fun at the wealthy, for although he was a firm believer in the rights of blue-blood breeding he had no time for upstarts. Self-made millionaires were rarely shown as shining members of the human race, and his portrayal of Vernon-Smith's father is a classic example of this, suggesting, as it does, that they lived on ill-gotten gains.

As Frank Richards once said:

"It is my experience, and I believe everybody's, that — excepting the peasant-on-the-land class, which is the salt of the earth — the higher you go up in the social scale the better you find the manners, and the more fixed the principles."

Whether Frank Richards was a snob or not, he took pains in his stories to portray snobbery as one of the most distasteful vices in our community, and therefore the moral still came through.

Our author was certainly not averse to the inclusion of corporal punishment in his stories, and it was quite a regular practice for one of the bad hats to receive his just deserts at the end of Quelchy's cane. And the times that Gosling hauled a boy on his back to receive a Head's flogging are uncountable. It was firmly believed in those days that the way to a boy's soul was through the seat of his trousers.

When criticised by the late George Orwell for never allowing sex to enter the pages of *The Magnet* and *Gem*, Frank Richards was swift to reply:

"Sex certainly does enter uncomfortably into the experience of the adolescent, but surely the less he thinks about it at an early age the better. I am aware that, in these modern days, there are people who think that their children should be told things which, in my own childhood, no small person was allowed to hear. I disagree with this entirely. My own opinion is that such people generally suffer from disordered digestions, which cause their minds to take a nasty turn. They fancy they are realists when they are only obscene. They go grubbing in the sewers for their realism and refuse to believe in the grass and flowers above ground — which — nevertheless — are equally real! Moreover, this 'motif' does not play so stupendous a part in real life, among healthy and wholesome people, as these realists imagine."

Frank Richards' greatest tenet was that his stories should not purposely feature the darker side of life. The possible blackness of the future should be ignored in his world of fantasy. His job was to entertain and generate happiness, and he had a very fine adage:

"Let youth be happy, or as happy as possible.

Happiness is the best preparation for misery, if misery must come. At least the poor kid will have had something! He may, at twenty, be hunting for a job and not finding it — why should his fifteenth year be clouded by worrying about that in advance? He may, at thirty, get the sack — why tell him so at twelve? He may, at forty, be a wreck on labour's scrapheap — but how will it benefit him to know that at fourteen? Even if making children miserable would make adults happy it would not be justifiable. But the truth is that the adult will be all the more miserable as a child. Every day of happiness, illusory or otherwise — and most happiness is illusory — is much to the good. It will help the boy to gain confidence and hope."

CHAPTER SEVENTEEN

the end of The Magnet and Gem

When in May 1940 *Magnet* No. 1684 *The Battle of the Beaks* failed to make its appearance despite being advertised the previous week, Greyfriars readers were left in a state of suspense similar to that which had gripped those who had delved into *The Mystery of Edwin Drood* in an earlier age.

The Shadow of the Sack, Magnet 1683, had seen the very last issue of the famous paper, killed off by the hazards and hard times of war.

This unfinished series dealt with Harry Wharton being suspected of some misdeed, and with Mr Quelch standing by his Form Captain, much to the annoyance of Mr Hacker of the Shell.

Apart from the number mentioned above, the other stories in hand were:

> 1685, *The Meddler* (originally titled *Bandy Bunter*)
> 1686, *What Happened to Hacker*
> 1687, *The Hidden Hand*

Soon after his paper closed down, the editor, C.M. Down, put these unpublished stories in a large box with other office files and records and handed them over to Harold J. Garrish, a Director of the Amalgamated Press, who in turn died suddenly in harness many years later. When his personal effects were sorted out it would appear that the stories had been destroyed, and so what actually transpired in the last Harry Wharton series was lost for ever.

"Billy Bunter was certainly not selling at his best during the last five or six years of his run," said Mr C.M. Down a little later in an interview. "When newsprint became scarce it was decided that many of the boys' papers and comics would have to go. They carried the least advertisements and therefore were receiving less revenue. *The Champion* type of papers did have a much larger circulation and obviously made far more money. That is why they were kept on, and Billy Bunter had to go."

In fact, *Magnet* sales had slumped alarmingly over the years from over 200,000 copies sold of each issue down to an average of 41,660 copies sold weekly during the last six months of its life. This is contrary to the general belief that it was a successful paper right to the end and would have run for years more.

The plain fact of the matter was that *The Magnet* was on probation until July 1940. And if sales hadn't picked up by then it would have been incorporated, in any case, in another paper.

Since the early thirties all sorts of ideas had been tried in attempts to boost circulation — to no avail. The editor was repeatedly hauled over the coals by his Controlling Editor and forced to attend Directors' Conferences to explain the reasons for the low sales. Things were far from happy on the Companion Papers' staff.

At one of these conferences, Down was shown a copy of a D.C. Thomson school story paper, *The Hotspur*. Said the editor afterwards with contempt in his voice: "I was appalled. Many of the stories were utter drivel and complete trash. I would have sooner resigned than asked Frank Richards to stoop to write such rubbish. Maybe they sell a few hundred thousand a week, but I have always had a sense of duty in providing good, clean wholesome school stories for boys. Later I mentioned the paper and one of the sensational stories to Mr Richards and he heartily agreed with me. I seem to recall that he made a sly dig at the story in one of his

Greyfriars yarns."

This is, of course, not the time nor the place to debate the merits or otherwise of D.C. Thomson boys' papers, but it is interesting to note that Frank Richards would seem to have taken a more humorous view of them than C.M. Down. When, in *Magnet* No. 1566 (1938) Wharton tries to seize a sensational boys' paper Bunter is reading:

> "You jolly well let that alone," exclaimed Bunter warmly. "I haven't finished reading it yet. I say, you fellows, it's a jolly good story — all about a boarding school for burglars, with the Headmaster a crook, and the assistant masters all convicts. A true-life story, you know . . ."

Frank Nugent eventually tries to get hold of the paper, not for perusal, but to tear up for scent in a paper chase!

Many of the old readers of *The Magnet* may recall an editorial message in the *Come into the Office Boys and Girls* column in the last issue but one:

> "An important announcement that will appeal to every one of you will be made shortly."

But alas, next week they were doomed to disappointment, as in the very last *Magnet* to be published they read:

> "In my last week's chat to you fellows I mentioned that an important announcement was to be made in this issue of *The Magnet*. For several weeks I have been working at top pressure on a scheme that would have appealed to every boy and girl. In fact, all preparations have been made, and the machinery was to be set in motion this week. Unfortunately, however, the acute paper shortage has forced me to postpone the scheme until some future date. To put you wise now as to what it actually was would only tend to spoil the pleasant surprise that is in store for you — and you would not like me to do this, would you? Rest assured it will not suffer in any way for the keeping."

The postponed announcement did not relate to free gifts, as most readers probably assumed, but to a last desperate attempt to attract new readership by means of a Billy Bunter Club.

Membership was to have been open to readers throughout the world, with a membership certificate and a badge in the likeness of the Fat Owl. Chief officers were to have been appointed in every major town and city, and the object was to have created a worldwide brotherhood. Officers and members would be expected to enrol new readers — which was the object of the entire exercise, thought up by a sales manager at Fleetway House.

C.H. Chapman had already completed several sketches to advertise the Club, and membership was also to be made available to readers of the comic *Knockout*, where Chapman had again been portraying Bunter in strip form. But it was not to be. *The Magnet* died, and the Club was still-born.

Roy Nash, a British film critic, writing in the wartime Middle-East forces newspaper *The Gen*, had this to say:

The Passing of Billy Bunter

Bunter is dead. The exact hour of his passing I know not, but I mourn him none the less for that. Looking through a pile of magazines in a bookshop the other morning I came upon a paper of incendiary hue known, with becoming modesty, as *The Knockout*. A note on the cover informed its readers that with it was incorporated *The Magnet*. Dry up your pool and you lose your fish. Chop down your oak tree and you have no acorns. Knock out your *Magnet* and you kill your Bunter . . .

It is true that *The Knockout* carries a comic strip chronicling the adventures of a well-built school-boy who bears Bunter's name. But compared with the Billy we used to know this young gentleman is a pale, N.A.A.F.I. teacake of a character. The true, the original Bunter was altogether too rich and too ripe a personality to be confined within the narrow frame of a comic strip. This is obviously an impostor . . .

. . . Bunter was a glorious creation, half clown, half rogue, a junior Pickwick with a dash of Falstaff . . . With him dies something of our youth."

After Chapman had ceased to draw *The Knockout* Billy Bunter strip another artist took over of whom it was maliciously said that he used to sweep the roads outside Fleetway House until somebody gave him a job with a pencil.

After the Lord Mayor's Show of *The Magnet, The Knockout* could only ever be regarded as being the dustcart.

The four unpublished *Magnet* stories were planned to be used later in a humorous magazine, said C.M. Down. But what he meant he never made clear. If it was a new project it never got further than the drawing board. But according to one Director of the Amalgamated Press it was probably intended to be *The Knockout*, in which case *The Magnet* stories would perforce have had to have been drastically cut.

If this was the case it was perhaps just as well that the stories instead slipped away into oblivion.

Perhaps it needs to be explained that the Amalgamated Press in those days had many subsidiaries, which included Canadian paper mills — the source of their own raw material. These mills were very profitable, and made more than enough money to cover any small losses incurred in Amalgamated Press publishing operations. Consequently there were cases of prestige papers being produced and just breaking even, or making a slight loss, and being subsidised by the profit from the mills, or from other papers.

It would be fair to say that *The Magnet,* although regarded as a prestige paper, was still making a profit each week, but only a small one. And even the desire for prestige has its limits. When a large convoy of ships carrying paper intended for the Amalgamated Press printing works was sunk out in the Western Approaches of the Atlantic the old familiar school of Greyfriars had to go.

If *Magnet* sales had caused some concern down the years, the state of *The Gem* was far worse. Frank Richards wrote just after the war:

> "That hapless paper had many queer vicissitudes and the duds had a fair field, with the result that they reduced the circulation to zero. The journal was saved by repeating the series from the beginning, but when these numbers were exhausted

> it would have to go. But then Martin Clifford was
> requested to resume, and he did so . . ."

The actual sales of *The Gem* in its last years were on
average only 15,800 copies a week. It had been even lower
than this before the reprints began. Frank Richards was
absolutely correct. Sales had reached rock bottom. It was left
to a Mr Eric Fayne, a Headmaster in Surrey who was greatly
concerned with the poor quality of the stories, to suggest
that they could not do better than to reprint the series from
the beginning.

At first his suggestion was turned down flat, but his
persistence eventually won the day. A desire for economy
probably came into the calculation as well. Using reprints
saved the payment of £38 to an author and more cash to an
artist. And so *The Gem* was saved.

Sales picked up slightly, but the paper could never expect
to regain its former glory. The reprints probably went on far
too long. It was almost eight years before any new stories
came from the real Martin Clifford.

According to official records, sales of *The Magnet* had
always been higher than those of *The Gem,* though there was
a time in the early days when St. Jim's almost caught up with
Greyfriars.

A possible explanation of the superior popularity of *The
Magnet* was given by a chief sub-editor on the staff of the
Companion Papers:

> "As to the fact that *The Magnet's* circulation was
> higher than that of *The Gem*: one of the reasons
> for this was that boys had more pocket money
> available on Mondays than Wednesdays. In those
> days pocket money was strictly limited, and many
> boys could only afford the luxury of one weekly
> paper. *The Magnet,* coming out earlier in the week,
> was their automatic choice."

When the genuine Martin Clifford returned to write new
stories for the paper he seemed determined to make his series
as long drawn-out as possible. Perhaps to prevent any of
'those wretched impostors' from creeping in again.

The Silverson series, which was actually the last to appear in *The Gem* just went on and on and on, until readers began to write in with irritation to enquire how much longer it would all last.

The supreme quality of readability was still there, of course. The author had not lost his powers as a story-teller. But the series was too long by far. It finally came to an end after a record seventeen instalments.

> "And it's going to be ripping next term at St. Jim's!" Tom Merry declared.
>
> "What-ho!" agreed Manners and Lowther.

"Hurry!" probably cried what readers were left . . . and then they read that next week they were asked to buy *The Triumph* instead of *The Gem*.

Curiously, Frank Richards had also drawn out the *Lamb series* in *The Magnet* far longer than necessary. Eight was always regarded as the ideal number of parts in a series. After this the reader was likely to become progressively more impatient for the denouement.

Did Frank Richards prolong his last series deliberately, knowing what the final denouement would be, sensing that the writing was on the wall for both of the papers?

That we will now never know.

CHAPTER EIGHTEEN

the dark years of war

With both of his papers closed down, the Amalgamated press either could not, or would not, use Frank Richards' proven talents and find him another outlet.

By the agreement of 1921 he had sold all rights in his characters, including Billy Bunter, to the Amalgamated Press. Now, when they refused to allow him to sell new stories of Greyfriars and St. Jim's elsewhere, his state of mind can be imagined.

On the other hand, the Directors of the Amalgamated Press were never quite as black-hearted as the author frequently painted them. They had paid him quite a large sum of money in 1921 to ensure that his characters only appeared in stories published by them. Now they were prepared to sell their rights to any other firm interested. What they were not prepared to do was simply hand them back to the author. In their view it was simply not good business.

The war was just gathering momentum after the 'phoney war' period. The unfortunate author, half blind, evacuated from his Kentish home and with his income rudely reduced to just five pounds a week from a honorarium paid him for the use of Billy Bunter in the comic strip in *The Knockout*, was left to seethe with resentment.

Not only were his lifelong writing habits brought to an abrupt end, but his heart was full of bitterness over his sudden impoverishment and what he considered to be the rank ingratitude that had brought it about. Like a liverish Mr Quelch at breakfast-time, he was understandably not at his best nor his most just.

One cannot but feel sorry for Frank Richards at this point in his life, for although he had earlier reached a certain pinnacle of prosperity he had spent freely and failed to make any provision for his old age. A newspaper report in the early days of the war announced that he was reduced to smoking dried rose leaves as he could not afford tobacco, which serves to accentuate the plight he had reached.

Where then did his money go? It is manifest that he was a steady, sober, clean-living gentleman who certainly never mixed with the bohemian Amalgamated Press writers who were wont to congregate in the Fleet Street taverns. For instance, one such author, Gwyn Evans in the Sexton Blake field, is reputed to have squandered £3,000 in a week — money received from film rights of one of his novels!

Perhaps Frank Richards had continued gambling even after his early experiences. Certainly his stories about the green tables of Monte Carlo were not all imagination. Frank Richards was not based entirely on Frank Nugent, but probably contained also a touch of Vernon-Smith!

To quote Frank Richards:

> A man who 'blues' fifty pounds a day is living at the rate of about twenty thousand a year. Even if it only lasts for one day, for that day he is a millionaire. When it has lasted a week, you begin to wonder — at least Frank Richards did — how many pages of typescript you will have to turn off the machine to get your finances in order again. When it lasts a month you pack up and go —.

Frank Richards, having reached the end of a normal man's working life, had finished up with almost nothing except the satisfaction of creation.

It was just after the war that he made the first draft of his Autobiography, which must have been vastly more exciting than the version which was eventually to find its way into print.

He had a large number of chips on his shoulder, and a number of blunt axes to grind, and he dealt faithfully with them according to his then somewhat vitriolic frame of mind. The strange eventful history of the *School Friend* was one irritation on which he spoke out, and another resulted in a long unfair piece on John Nix Pentelow.

Other chapters dealt with the iniquities of the Amalgamated Press, substitute writers and even the editors who encouraged them. Frank Richards then said:

> About the Autobiography, a good many difficulties have cropped up, partly owing to Frank being too frank, if I may so express it: and so it is still in the state of Amfortas in *Parsifal:* neither alive nor dead. Frank Richards does not feel disposed to blot a single line of it: having taken Hotspur's advice to heart to 'tell the truth and shame the devil'.

In the end, however, on maturer thought, and influenced by soothing advice, he cooled down and excised the rancorous sections. The devil remained unshamed, but the book reached print eventually in 1952, whereas in its original form it stood the chance of standing on too many corns to achieve that happy state. Aware of the laws of libel, no publisher would entertain it until its more lurid and less than just denunciations had been toned down.

It is a truism that many an author, upon hitting hard times, will lay the blame on the lack of percipience of his readers or if this, on sober reflection, seems too absurd, will lash out at his publishers. By some mental gymnastic he will ignore the fact that it is his publishers who have taken most of the financial risks; that it is his publishers who will sometimes produce at a loss, rather than let down their hardworking but often ungrateful author. The author, more than artists in most other fields, is subject to hubris of sometimes scarifying dimensions.

The Autobiography of Frank Richards was praised to the skies by a select band of faithful followers, who believed he could do no wrong, but the general public and majority of his old readers could not have been more disappointed. It seemed that all the chapters one wanted to read had been left out.

Frank Richards wrote the book about Frank Richards, who cannot be identified with Charles Hamilton as, according to our author, each is a different person and merge but here and there.

This was a most irritating book in many ways, and its opening line — *Frank Richards, at seventeen . . .* — must have disappointed all his followers immediately. Why his publishers did not insist on his full life story is a mystery as deep and as baffling as why he was indulged to devote chapter after chapter to the trivialities of his holidays abroad. In brief, the autobiography could be said to be a pretty successful attempt to avoid writing about things that any reader would want to know.

Frank Richards' public acclaim could be said to have started in October, 1943. Wanting a feature article in hand to cover future slack dates, the London *Evening Standard* interviewed Frank Richards, identifying him at the same time as Martin Clifford, Owen Conquest, etc. The man, in other words, responsible for all those stories of school life. The number of letters Frank Richards subsequently received was staggering. Hundreds came from old readers, continuing to pour in later from all parts of the world. Old *Magnet* and *Gem* readers corresponded and got together; Old Boys' Book Clubs were formed, starting in London, branching out to all parts of the United Kingdom, and later throughout the Commonwealth.

Since the beginning of the war a small magazine called *Story Paper Collector* had been published by Bill Gander in Transcona, Manitoba, Canada. Then, in 1946, the *Collectors' Digest* was launched by a Yorkshireman, Herbert Leckenby, and later, on his death, taken over by Eric Fayne of Surbiton — the same Headmaster who had suggested the *Gem* reprints. These Book Clubs received much publicity on radio and TV, and the national newspapers especially were never slow to write about the high prices demanded for old copies of the

Magnet and *Gem.* Publicity was meat and drink to Frank Richards and he owed a great deal to the *Collectors' Digest* and the Old Boys' Book Clubs for making his name a household word.

That Frank Richards showed his affection and appreciation to his loyal band of followers is beyond question. However large his mail bag he never failed to answer letters. One Christmas he received over five hundred greetings, and there is no doubt he carried out his vow to answer every one of them personally.

The paper shortage had killed off most of the periodical publishers during the war, except for the larger ones who were bringing out thin fortnightly editions. However, in 1944, Frank Richards was able to get his new school, Carcroft, accepted in Hutchinsons' smart little magazine *Pie.*[1]

A successful wartime publisher, Mr Gerald Swan, remembers Frank Richards ringing him up and offering to do a new school series. But they could not agree on terms, and so the project fell through. Mr Swan paid the same rates to all writers, but Frank Richards wanted more. Obviously his business acumen — or his need — had increased since his Amalgamated Press days.

Frank Richards also found that publishers still wanted Billy Bunter and Greyfriars, but he simply could not agree to their requests because of the Amalgamated Press copyright. When a reader queried his motive for writing of Carcroft for *Pie* instead of Greyfriars, he replied:

> Billy Bunter is gone forever, as I have completely severed my connections with the Amalgamated Press, and these people claim — by what right I cannot say — to prohibit me from writing Greyfriars stories for any other publisher. I am getting a little too old to enter into a legal wrangle, so I

---

1 Very reminiscent of Greyfriars, this was made up of three boys Compton, Drake and Lee, along with the new Vernon-Smith — this time called Dudley Vane-Carter, or V.C. for short, and based on Percy Griffith. The author also acquired a new status in *Pie* by compiling the Frank Richards Crossword Puzzle.

Many other pot-boiler schools for small firms followed, including Sparshott, Headland House, Topham, Lynwood, Tipdale, High Lynn, Barcroft, Felgate and St. Kate's. In an attempt to boost slow sales some of these carried the by-line 'The Author of the Billy Bunter Stories'.

decided to begin something entirely new. Perhaps after so long a run it was time for Harry Wharton & Co to make their final bow and retire from the scene.

Arthur Garfain, an Australian publisher, found himself confronted by the same copyright quandary. As an old reader of the *Magnet* and *Gem* he wanted Richards to write a series of Greyfriars stories for his new boys' paper in Australia, *The Silver Jacket*. Eventually, of course, he had to settle for Carcroft.

When Frank Richards wrote off Bunter and Harry Wharton it was with a feeling of despair, and he resigned himself to the fact that these brain children who had satisfied his purse for so many years were lost to him.

But the publisher Charles Skilton of Wimbledon was soon to alter all that, and renewed publicity eventually brought Bunter back into millions of homes.

CHAPTER NINETEEN

Bunter post war — star of books, television & stage

When Frank Richards left Monty Haydon's office in Fleetway House one day late in 1946 he was feeling highly elated. His resentment against the Amalgamated Press had been swept away as if by magic and, once more — to quote his favourite phrase — 'All was calm and bright'.

Monty Haydon had given him permission, ex gratia, to write new Greyfriars stories, but only to be published in hardback form by the publisher Charles Skilton.

Probably the Amalgamated Press had realised that in magazine story form Greyfriars and Billy Bunter had lost their potential in the brave new world of post-war publishing. The days had gone for ever when *The Magnet* could sell profitably with a circulation of only 40,000 copies. In these days large circulations were essential to survival.

And it wasn't only the economics of juvenile publishing which had changed. So had the style. Words were out and pictures were in.[1]

So, after fifty years of writing, Frank Richards would for the first time have the distinction of appearing in hard covers. And also for the first time his stories would be available in public libraries.

[1] When in 1950 Reginald Eves revived *The School Friend* as a new style picture-story weekly it sold over a million copies weekly, a record for any boys' or girls' publication with the possible exception of Hulton Press's *Eagle*.

Working out the length of his first hardbacked book at roughly the same as that of two *Magnet* stories, Frank Richards amazed Charles Skilton by asking for payment at the rate of thirty shillings a thousand words, which was not much different from what he was getting in Amalgamated Press days before the war. Being a fair man, Mr Skilton eventually persuaded him to accept a contract on a royalty basis. In consequence, for the first story in the series, aptly entitled *Billy Bunter of Greyfriars School,* he eventually received over £1,000 — almost ten times as much as he had expected.

Probably of all the post-war Bunter books the first was the closest to being an original story, for many of the others were simply unashamed rehashes of earlier *Magnet* tales. All of the books revolved around Bunter, of course. He was the central character. It was he that the publisher and the public demanded.

Whilst it may be perfectly true to say that these Bunter Books were written for a new generation, it is also a fact that it was the 'old faithfuls' who publicised them and helped to make them so successful.

On the other hand, for the old *Magnet* reader there was nothing outstanding about the quality of the stories in the 'Bunter Books.' Nevertheless, they enjoyed a very steady market.

After some years of publishing them at the rate of two titles a year, Charles Skilton sold the contract to Cassells who continued to publish up to and after Frank Richards' death in 1961.

It was rather ironic that the last pair were based on old TV scripts found amongst Frank Richards' effects and written up probably by one of 'those wretched impostors'.

Mandeville Publications decided in 1949 that what Bunter could do, D'Arcy could do better, and ran stories of Tom Merry in hardback, and also in Annual form.

Skilton replied with yet another old favourite — Bessie Bunter of Cliff House — the first story that the original Hilda

Richards had written for thirty years.

Further publicity was given to Frank Richards in the West of England when *The Bristol Evening World* reprinted an old *Magnet* story in serial form — *The Mystery of Study No. 1*

It would appear that with the success of the Bunter Books the Amalgamated Press had had second thoughts about reprinting the Greyfriars stories and had decided that there was life in Billy Bunter yet. So *Comet* started one page stories by the genuine Frank Richards as an experiment, and this was followed much later by a series of St. Jim's tales in the companion paper, *Sun.* The man behind both moves was Leonard Matthews, who had worked under Monty Haydon, and was likewise a great creative force.

The Tom Merry stories were, however, updated to some extent by the editor, Alfred Wallace, and old St. Jim's readers must have been surprised to find modern slang expressions cropping up in dialogue — such as "Whizzo" and other non-Martin Clifford exclamations.

Both series were eventually dropped as they brought little response from regular readers, and the only comments seem to have come from old *Gem* addicts. Edward Holmes, a group editor, simply said:

> "The series are being discontinued due to the poor response from the modern generation of readers. It is the publishers' belief that the undoubted interest in the Greyfriars and St. Jim's stories was a nostalgic one."

But the main factor really was that the stories were far too short for the author to develop any plot or style.

By 1952 Frank Richards could be said to have reached the pinnacle of his career, for that was the year in which Billy Bunter appeared on B.B.C. Television.

When, earlier, in December 1951 the B.B.C. had announced that it wanted a Billy Bunter for a new children's programme no less than seventy-five porky hopefuls, most wearing glasses and of rotund appearance applied for the part.

The newspapers naturally made great play of this and when the subsequent choice was 29-year-old Gerald Campion, a small-time actor, married with two children and who tipped the scales at a mere 11 stone 12 pounds, his selection was received with very mixed feelings.

Joy Harrington, in charge of the series, had been given a well-nigh impossible task, for to recreate the famous fat boy and the equally famous school was tempting fate. Obviously she couldn't please or satisfy everyone, least of all the Old Guard, and it was inevitable that the reception accorded the first episode on February 19th 1952, *The Siege of the Remove,* should be as mixed as that given the choice of Bunter himself.

The experienced seniors were not too badly portrayed, and Kynaston Reeves as Mr Quelch did at times get near to the part. There were also moments of genius in Gerald Campion's portrayal, although he was, in the main, likened to the early Bunter.

But the other boys! A colourless Harry Wharton, a mere member of the Greek Chorus; an incredible Inky repeating a few of his flowery lines without any expression at all. A Bob Cherry who said "Hallo! Hallo! Hallo!" now and again like a parrot. Worst of all was a dreadful caricature of the steady and steadfast Wingate, captain of the school.

Just before television closed down on the evening before the first broadcast, viewers were shown a short film of an interview given by Frank Richards at his home to Miss Joy Harrington and Mr C.H. Chapman. The announcer held a *Magnet* cover before the camera whilst announcing the film — an excellent introduction to the television series of Greyfriars plays and tantalising to those who dearly remembered the characters.

Frank Richards' comments on the series were:

"Bunter on TV seems to have roused a lot of comment. For myself I can only repeat that I like it very much indeed. If it isn't quite perfect, is anything in this imperfect world? I just love watching the plays and wish they would go on for ever."

Jonah Barrington, radio critic of the *Sunday Chronicle* said that his readers regarded Billy Bunter as the greatest T.V. character since Muffin the Mule, a comparison not destined to please old readers of *Magnet*, but at least saying something in favour of the production.

There was also, sadly, a certain emptiness about the sets, and it does seem that the plays were produced on a shoestring budget. Apart from the Famous Five, Bunter and one or two other characters, the school seemed completely deserted. A few boy extras would have done wonders to recreate the hustle and bustle of a real school.

Nevertheless, the TV series was watched by children, for that was its main purpose, and even if adults did cringe it certainly furthered the claim that Bunter was the world's most famous schoolboy and Frank Richards the greatest living school story writer.

However, to satisfy some of the older generation, the B.B.C. screened these plays on both children's and the older children's evening programmes, to enable Dad to have a sneaky view.

The same year Frank Richards also produced what was easily his best writing since his early *Gem* days. This was when Goldhawk Books of Shepherds Bush, and whose offices were in a block of flats in Goldhawk Road, produced a series of eleven paperbacks. These were really excellent reading, and it was a great pity that they were not better distributed.

By this time Frank Richards had also brought out a new character, whom he obviously thought a lot of — Jack of All Trades. And our author was just as busy as he had been in the golden pre-war days of *The Magnet* and *Gem*.

The second Bunter series on TV was much better than the first. The production team had obviously learned a little from the first six episodes. This time there was a new cast to portray The Famous Five, and Gerald Campion had improved tremendously, and actually looked and acted the part. This was easily the best performance he had given in his acting career until that time.

Almost half a century after Billy Bunter had first appeared in *The Magnet*, the Fat Owl of the Remove made his debut on the London West End stage. The Producer was an old *Magnet* reader, Maurice McLoughlin. The first show was presented at the Palace Theatre, matinees only, and was put on by City Stage Productions Limited, headed by Michael Anthony and Bernadette Milnes. Gerald Campion, now 35, played Bunter on stage, and with years of Bunter TV appearances behind him he was the obvious selection.

The Bunter Christmas shows were popular and far superior to the TV productions. They continued as a yearly affair with *Billy Bunter Flies East, Billy Bunter's Swiss Roll, Billy Bunter Shipwrecked, Billy Bunter's Christmas Circus* and *Billy Bunter Meets Magic* — featuring David Nixon.

Later shows, though still written by McLoughlin (who died a few years ago) were staged at the Queens Theatre and the Victoria Palace with Peter Bridgmont playing the part of Billy Bunter. Gerald Campion played in a Scottish production. At one of these early shows in London, there, playing the piano, was Eric Fayne, surely the world's most loyal Greyfriars and St. Jim's enthusiast.

With his re-establishment now complete, Frank Richards was able to let much of his incidental work fall by the wayside. He had brought out a winner in a *Billy Bunter Annual*, but he had also come to the conclusion that St. Jim's, Rookwood and Cliff House were little in demand.

Receiving half of the fees paid for the TV and Christmas plays copyright — the other half of which went to the Amalgamated Press — he settled down to write a couple of Bunter books each year for the rest of his life.

His output at the end of his days — though not bearing comparison with the hectic pre-war era — was still a formidable one for a man of such elderly years.

This man who had made and lost several fortunes never knew the meaning of the word retirement — for he was still working right up to the very end.

CHAPTER TWENTY

exit the master

In his declining years, Frank Richards became more and more of a recluse, seeing few visitors, except children – whom he loved all his life – or very close family friends.

If in an awkward or a grumpy mood, and not wishing to see certain visitors, he would retire to his bed and declare he was ill. Yet despite the natural idiosyncrasies of someone feeling their age he still answered his vast number of correspondents with courtesy and cheerfulness. His letters were still typed in the familiar mauve print, with the large black ink signature written as firmly as ever.

One of his very last callers was a correspondent of a national newspaper, and he described Frank Richards vividly thus:

"He sat by the fire – a frail old man, and he smiled a toothless smile. His small, frail body began at the top, under a small black skull cap, and ended on the floor in a pair of soft carpet slippers. The rest of him was wrapped up in a crumpled dressing gown."

Other visitors found him inclined to ramble a bit, and change quickly from one subject to another, evading the point in question:

"I'm a little like Bunter: I like puddings and sweets." "I'm a very old man, I can't last much longer. It's absurd to worry about death. When death comes, why, I feel it will be like changing trains on a long train journey. That's all there is to it."

"Did you read in the newspapers, they want Englishmen to emigrate to Australia. I'm thinking of doing this. After all, I'm still young in spirit, and I've lived a quiet, sober life."

"I only watched the Bunter shows on television — and Richard Dimbleby. What a fine big man he was, reminded me of Hinton. What a tragic end to old Figgins."

"I shall be writing about boys till the very end. A boy can see through humbug quicker than any man." "Did you ask about Alonzo Todd? Yes, I think he did leave Greyfriars because of poor health, and went to stay with his Uncle Benjamin."

"I think a lot about God, and the life to come. Did you know I once wrote a book on religion, but no publisher would buy it. All they wanted was Bunter."

A few days before Christmas, when he died peacefully in his sleep, it is believed that he went completely blind, and death was probably a merciful release, as his whole world and life was in writing about the boys he loved so well.

He was cremated at Charing, in Kent, some thirty miles from his home at Kingsgate, on a day which, by some strange twist of fate, was typical of one of his school story settings.

White snow and ice lay everywhere in this part of the beautiful Kentish countryside. The crematorium itself looked almost like Wharton Lodge in the wintry background, with its snow covered drive and lovely avenue of frosty old trees.

And so Frank Richards, the most loved school story writer of all time, returned to dust.

Greyfriars, however, still goes on in its unchanging way, for it is a place without a calendar, and time has stood still there for over sixty years.

The passage of time leaves the old school unscathed, despite its floggings, expulsions, barring-outs, japes and perilous foreign tours. The Famous Five, and Bunter of course, return safe and sound on every occasion, to start a new term of who knows what adventures.

Angular Mr Quelch, a beast but a just beast, is still writing the history of Greyfriars, with one gimlet eye still fixed on the restless members of the Remove. Plump, portly Mr Paul Prout is still 'jawing' in the Masters' Common Room about how he shot a grizzly bear with a small bore rifle way out West in the Rockies, in the 1890s.

Skinner, Snoop and Stott continue to have a quiet smoke behind the woodshed or in the Remove box-room. Gay Blades, Black Sheep, Cads and Bounders still leave their school-caps by the wooden palings of The Three Fishers or Cross Keys to be spotted by a master or prefect. Beery, unshaven, foul-mouthed tramps with cudgels continue to lurk the leafy lanes around Friardale Wood.

Florid-faced Joey Banks with his loud checked suit still gives racing certs to Gerald Loder of the Sixth, whilst Inky of The Famous Five still speaks in his flowery language despite his expensive Greyfriars public school education.

What a haven of refuge is Greyfriars from the troubled, inflated, mad, mad world we live in today. Maybe it is a Peter Pan illusion of eternal youth, but what better memorial could Frank Richards have than this?

CHAPTER TWENTY ONE

epilogue

> "Frank Richards . . . a bad writer? He had a strange
> genius that grasped something true and essential
> about the British character, and could transfer it
> into his stories. This is a power that many more
> 'respectable' writers might envy."

So wrote Colin Wilson in the *Daily Express* in his tribute
to Frank Richards after the announcement of his
death. Wilson meant what he said about the author's genius
but only referred to him in the writing context after
reference to remarks made by George Orwell in an article on
boys' weeklies published in 1940.

Orwell had said that Frank Richards was hopelessly
out-of-date, that his writing was atrocious, that all of his
characters were stereotyped and that most of his values were
false. Ironically, the cultural magazine *Horizon* in which
Orwell's article appeared is no longer popularly remembered
but Billy Bunter and The Famous Five go on for ever.

Needless to say, Frank Richards did not allow Orwell's
remarks to go unanswered and in a subsequent article he
dissected Orwell's attack, piece by piece, and thoroughly
destroyed his argument.

One leading writer of Greyfriars and St. Jim's substitute

stories, George Samways, had his own view of The Master, as
he called him:

> "When I was asked some time ago if I considered
> Frank Richards the greatest writer of school stories
> I replied that I should call him the best loved,
> rather than the greatest. That seemed to me then —
> and still seems to me now — a very high tribute,
> which should satisfy even the most rabid Richards
> partisan.
>
> It is true to say that Frank Richards' stories
> varied a great deal in style and quality. He did not
> write at the same high level all the time. For all his
> genius he was human. Did he not have his off days,
> like any other writer? Was he never down with flu,
> or racked with toothache, causing him to write
> below his best? If a poor story got by it was due to
> the fact that Frank Richards' manuscripts were
> hastily read by sub-editors or proof readers and
> were sent to the printers without amendments of
> any sort. One came to trust his stories, and in times
> of pressure the manuscripts were often sent to the
> printers without any perusal whatsoever. Frank
> Richards was highly thought of in the editorial
> office."

How does one determine whether an author is a good or a
bad one? Does one decide by an analysis of the literary value
of the prose, or by the quality of the language employed, or
the dynamic nature of the plot? Or does one simply decide
on entertainment value?

The mere fact that a man is described as an author is not,
in itself, any assurance of literacy. John W. Bobin, otherwise
known as 'Mark Osborne', an early Sexton Blake author, sent
out from his laundry at Southend many stories written upon
scraps of paper. They were excellently plotted but needed
vigorous sub-editing, and particularly, attention to grammar,
before they could be printed.

How many times can one read a best-selling novel with the
same thrill and excitement as the first time? Not very often.
But with a Frank Richards story there is a difference. It can

be read a dozen times over a period and each time with the same interest and enjoyment.

This serves to prove just how good a writer Frank Richards really was. This was his genius. He could do what other writers could not, and create a story that could be read with pleasure again and again.

Frank Richards seems to have been most influenced by those two great Victorian writers Charles Dickens and Lewis Carroll, with perhaps passing an acknowledgement to W.S. Gilbert, of the well-loved Gilbert and Sullivan duo. Many years ago, a Professor at Cambridge classed Frank Richards' style of allowing his characterisations to completely dominate his storytelling the most exact parallel to Carroll and Dickens that he had ever seen.

Frank Richards did not usually paint a precise school scene; he left the pictorial detail of a situation to the reader, and this suited most readers' tastes. He did not describe the studies in detail, nor the school grounds, apart from making an occasional reference to some particular object of relevance. What he really concentrated on was character and dialogue, which was always lively and amusing. It is this which makes his stories so readable to adults, and he never wrote down to the level of the youngest reader, like so many other writers for boys.

His strong appeal to adult readers is evidenced by the success of W. Howard Baker's Greyfriars Press series of bound volumes of Magnet and Gem collections. Produced in superior fashion, exact facsimiles of the pre-war magazines, they sell to the widest range of adult readers from all walks of life[1] and from all parts of the world.

When asked how he made his characters come so much alive, Frank Richards explained that curiously since his eye accident and his extreme short sightedness, the boys seemed

1 A poll conducted on the subject recently showed that occupations include: doctors, chartered accountants, lawyers, airline pilots, industrial workers, postmen, miners, members of Parliament, university professors, college lecturers, schoolmasters and mistresses, army navy and air force officers and other ranks, artists, priests and ministers of every denomination, civil servants, bank managers, police officers, engineers, housewives, interior decorators, photographers, company directors, authors, journalists, musicians, film actors, architects, TV personalities, librarians, publishers, stock brokers and magicians.

to be real flesh and blood when he typed. He became so absorbed with them in his writing that he could actually hear their voices, visualise their actions, see the expressions on their faces. It would seem that nature, in its mysterious, wonderful and uncanny way had given him an extra sense to make up for his deficient eyesight.

Many highbrow critics of Frank Richards refused to recognise his talent simply because he was a mass producer of popular school story literature for unsophisticated young people.

Yet in his field Frank Richards was top of his class. Had he devoted his time to the mere production of one hardbacked novel every year, written in his brightest and best vein, probably more honour would have come his way. As it was, he left behind a legacy of many thousands of entrancing evergreen stories. No admirer would have wished him to do anything else.

A permanent memorial to him is to be found in The Charles Hamilton Museum, situated at 30, Tonbridge Road, Maidstone, Kent. Its curator is John Wernham, President of the London Old Boys Book Club. Since 1962, he has gradually built up a collection of original letters, manuscripts, photographs, and files of *Magnets* and *Gems* and other boys' papers containing Hamilton material. There are also C.H. Chapman drawings, and many personal effects belonging to the author.

Most people would agree that Frank Richards had a profound influence for good on the youth of Britain during the first half of this century. He taught a splendid moral code without the slightest suggestion of preaching or priggishness. He was a sensitive, gentle person who asked little and gave much.

He was a charming and scholarly gentleman of the old school whose standards of moral decency and professional workmanship were regrettably conspicuous by being so unusual in the world he left behind him on Christmas Eve, in the Year of Our Lord nineteen hundred and sixty-one.

APPENDIX 1

Full List of Charles Hamilton's Pen-names.

Winston Cardew	Romance Series (W.C. Merrett)
Martin Clifford	Popular (1st and 2nd); B.F.L. (1st); Pluck (2nd); Gem (1st and 2nd); Marvel (2nd); Triumph; Boys Friend Weekly (2nd); Schoolboys Own Library; Empire Lib (2nd); Greyfriars Holiday Annual; Goldhawk Books.
Harry Clifton	Chuckles
Clifford Clive	School and Sport
Sir Alan Cobham	Modern Boy (1st) (Ghosted)
Owen Conquest	Popular (1st and 2nd); Boys Friend Weekly (2nd); Gem (2nd); Magnet; Schoolboy Own Lib; B.F.L. (1st); Greyfriars Herald (2nd); Greyfriars Holiday Annual; Knockout.
Gordon Conway	Vanguard Lib; Funny Cuts; Vanguard Lib.
Freeman Fox	Coloured Comic; Worlds Comic
Hamilton Greening	Funny Cuts
Cecil Herbert	Vanguard Lib; Picture Fun
Prosper Howard	Chuckles; Empire Lib (1st and 2nd); B.F.L. (1st); Gem (2nd)
Robert Jennings	Picture Fun

APPENDIX 1 (cont.)

Gillingham Jones	Picture Fun; Vanguard Lib; Funny Cuts
T Harcourt Llewelyn	Smiles
Clifford Owen	Diamond Lib (1st); Jacks Paper
Ralph Redway	Modern Boy (1st); Ranger (1st); Popular (2nd) B.F.L. (2nd)
Ridley Redway	Vanguard Lib; Funny Cuts; Picture Fun; Smiles
Frank Richards	Popular (1st and 2nd); Dreadnought; Ranger (1st and 2nd); Gem (2nd); Magnet. Boys Friend Weekly (2nd); B.F.L. (1st); Schoolboys Own Library; Chuckles; Greyfriars Holiday Annual; Knockout Fun Book; Tom Merry's Own; Billy Bunters Own; Mascot Schoolboy Series; Sparshott Series; Wonder Book of Comics; Silver Jacket, and other post war publications.
Hilda Richards	Schoolfriend (1st)
Raleigh Robbins	Funny Cuts
Robert Rogers	Funny Cuts; Picture Fun
Eric Stanhope	Vanguard Lib; Picture Fun
Robert Stanley	Vanguard Lib; Best Budget; Funny Cuts; Larks (Trapps Holmes)
Nigel Wallace	Vanguard Lib
Talbot Wynyard	Picture Fun

CHUMS OF LYNWOOD

by FRANK RICHARDS

3D.

AUTHOR OF THE FAMOUS
BILLY AND BESSIE BUNTER STORIES

EXCITING BOY & GIRL STORIES

I say, you fellows, old Bunter is 72!

OODLES of tuck (egg sandwiches, cake, and tarts) were laid out. The fire was a real crumpet-toaster. I was helping to celebrate the birthday of a fat, frabjous, foozling, frumptious fraud—who has also become a folk-hero of our island race, one of the most famous characters in English fiction.

Billy Bunter is 72.

"It's hard to think of Bunter as an elderly man, almost as ancient as I am." remarked his creator, Mr. Frank Richards, who at 84 still taps out his Greyfriars School epics at a steady 5,000 words a week. "But I first invented him for a story in 1899, and he was 14 to set out with."

As an early *Magnet* and *Gem* addict myself, I had with fascination driven down to Kingsgate in Kent to have tea with the legend-maker who has himself become a latterday legend.

His provider

ON the way I passed the huge lettering at Margate DREAM-LAND WELCOMES YOU. That seemed still to apply when I sat down with the tiny, cosy old dream-spinner in black skull cap, dressing-gown, scarf, stiff white collar, and bicycle clips functioning as draught-excluders around his brown corduroy slacks.

Filling a curved pipe from a tobacco jar, he observed : " You can't help having an affection for a companion of half-a-century. Besides, he is keeping me, so I should feel thankful for him. You wouldn't think of Bunter as a provider, would you ? "

For although Mr. Richards may continue to describe the Owl of the Remove as a fat tick, a fat grampus and a fat diddler, and record every yarooooooh of pain as he is jabbed with a boat-hook, bumped, or kicked down a flight of steps that would kill anyone except a folk-hero, he has cause for deep gratitude to Bunter.

For 20 years up to the last war, Charles Hamilton (his real name) was not only Frank Richards but Martin Clifford, Owen Conquest, Ralph Redway, and Hilda Richards.

All volcanically erupted one and a half million words a year about boys' and girls' schools as well as the serialised adventures of the Rio Kid, King of the Islands, and Herlock Sholmes.

For 30 years the Owl of the Remove helped his creator to earn yachts and champagne money... then came disaster ...and now once again Bunter is the Golden Boy

For all that, golden age he earned £2,500 a year, when that was yachts - and - champagne money, and that in dribs to another drama in the dorm was rattled off in Rome, Venice, and down the Riviera way.

Luck ran out

"**M**ONTE CARLO was my spiritual home," I heard with some astonishment, and I experienced a slight shock — as if I had caught Harry Wharton smoking a reefer — to learn that the merry japes of those clean-limbed, cricket-playing, viceless English school lads were bashed out between tough all-night sessions at the roulette table.

The luck ran out along with peace. War-time paper shortage killed off the *Magnet* and the *Gem.* At 70 the playboy bachelor found himself without income, without a home he was evicted from the coastal zones, and without savings, for shares bought for 30s. plummeted to 3s. 6d., and what was left went to pay back income tax.

"I have always been lucky, most of all in having a natural buoyancy," he said. "I was rather on the rocks, couldn't get anything published, but being left stranded didn't affect my spirits.

"I got a house in Hampstead Garden Suburb, and all those six years I used to go to my desk each morning and write my stint. I kept going.

Start again

"**T**HEN, when the war ended, it was a matter of starting again at 72. I've since sold pretty well everything I wrote during the war. And here we are again ! "

Where Frank Richards is again is on a high-earning crest. For a curious thing happened during the wartime blackout. A cult interest began to grow in those unearthly public schools populated by hearty Peter Pans destined never to grow up.

In *Horizon,* most egghead of reviews, George Orwell did a brilliant piece of social analysis

on the *Magnet* and other boys' weeklies, but Orwell took it for granted that no one person could have kept up such a tornado output for 30 years and that "Frank Richards" and "Martin Clifford" were house labels for the contributions of a multitude of hack journalists.

When Frank Richards wrote in to clear up that misapprehension, and revealed himself as the master-mind behind Bunter and Company, the documentation began really flying.

In the past 15 years the Famous Five and the pals of Remove have been honoured on the B.B.C. and written about in publications all over the world, including some serious dissection in *The Times Educational Supplement,* and *The Manchester Guardian.* Bibliophiles began dredging for old issues and data.

Then Frank Richards came full circle back to popularity on a wider scale than ever before.

Now Bunter is the prima donna. He dominates the titles of all 21 books that have come out from Cassells since the war (two a year, four on the stocks, and a quarter-million copies in print). He has his own Christmas annual (20,000 orders before printing this year). He even paraded in enormous effigy in the last Lord Mayor's Show.

And of course millions of children, watching Gerald Campion in the TV series, have relearned that curious facetious Edwardian slang ("benighted chump," "Oh, haddocks," and "Good egg!") that has throughout been a changeless incantation.

Indeed, that is part of the mystery of Frank Richards—that in this Welfare State age of social levelling, these stylised, repetitive stories of a sort of soft-drink Tom Brown's Schooldays, a never-never land of cads, monocles, titled fags, £5 hampers and "old grey s.ones," have obviously still got a strong, faintly snob glamour.

No copies

THE explanation is Bunter, a creation as monumentally comic as anything Dickens invented.

Frank Richards finished singing for me a Gilbert and Sullivan song in Latin (one of his hobbies) and presented me with the translation he had just finished typing.

"I don't need it," he explained. "I remember everything I've written, and I've never kept a copy in my life." And he added, with some regret : "But I do wish I'd kept all those thousands of *Magnets* which I always chucked away."

For those rare first editions of the adventures of Billy Bunter (price 1d.) now fetch 25s., a copy on the collectors' market.

Magnet artist C.H. Chapman.

APPENDIX 2

Frank Richards had been a great admirer of Conan Doyle's Sherlock Holmes stories, since he first read them as a young man in the *Strand Magazine*. When H.A. Hinton had launched *The Greyfriars Herald* in 1915, a novel idea of a school magazine, edited by Harry Wharton, and with contributions by the inhabitants of Greyfriars: Frank Richards was able to put his enthusiasm to good effect. Under the pen-name of 'Peter Todd', a member of the Remove, he penned a delightful series of parodies on the great Baker Street detective.

These were entitled "The Adventures of Herlock Sholmes", and featured Dr. Jotson, their home being at Shaker Street. Some early tales such as "The Bound of the Haskervilles", and "The Freckled Hand", were outstanding, and the stories ran for some time. Tales not used in this paper were eventually inserted in *The Magnet*, *Gem*, and *Penny Popular*, when some of the much later ones were penned by Stanton-Hope, and G.R. Samways. There were about 84 stories in all, and in recent years a cult seems to have been built up around them, and they are collected avidly, especially in America. Frank Richards own detective in his school stories of Greyfriars (and early St. Jim's) was Ferrers Locke, relation to Dr Locke Headmaster of the Kent school. Ferrers Locke and his assistant Jack Drake (formerly of Greyfriars) had, of course, to live at Baker Street, along with Sexton Blake and many other detectives of fiction.

THE GREYFRIARS HERALD (1st Series)

No.	Date	Title

THE ADVENTURES OF HERLOCK
SHOLMES by "Peter Todd"

No.	Date	Title
1.	20/11/1915	The Adventure of the Diamond Pins.
2.	27/11/1915	The Case of the Biscuit Tin.
3.	4/12/1915	The Bound of the Haskervilles.
4.	11/12/1915	The Freckled Hand.
5.	18/12/1915	The Sign of Fourty-Four.
6.	25/12/1915	The Death of Sholmes.
7.	1/ 1/1916	The Return of Herlock Sholmes.
8.	8/ 1/1916	The Missing Mother-in-law.
9.	15/ 1/1916	The Adventure of the Brixton Builder.
10.	22/ 1/1916	The Case of the American Millionaire.
11.	29/ 1/1916	The Foreign Spy.
12.	5/ 2/1916	The Case of the Pipe-Clay Department.
13.	12/ 2/1916	The Case of the Pawned Pickle-jar.
14.	19/ 2/1916	The Munition Mystery.
15.	26/ 2/1916	The Captured Submarines.
16.	4/ 3/1916	The Sham Huns.
17.	11/ 3/1916	The Kaiser's Code.
18.	18/ 3/1916	The Yellow Phiz.

End of Series. Revived in 1919.
commenced at No. 1. again.

First Herlock Sholmes tales in. . .

No.	Date	Title
33.	12/ 6/1920	The Missing Cricketer.
34.	19/ 6/1920	The Bacon Mystery.
35.	26/ 6/1920	The Chopstein Venus.
36.	3/ 7/1920	The Case of the Missing Heir.
37.	10/ 7/1920	The Mystery of the Studio.
38.	17/ 7/1920	The Case of the Musican.
39.	24/ 7/1920	The Mystery of the Taxi-Cab.
40.	31/ 7/1920	The Case of the Stolen Car.
41.	7/ 8/1920	The Case of the Ball Dress.
42.	14/ 8/1920	The Disappearance of Lord Adolphus.
43.	21/ 8/1920	The Mystery of the Garden Suburb.
44.	28/ 8/1920	The Case of the Sinn Feiners.

THE GREYFRIARS HERALD (cont.)

45.	4/ 9/1920	The Case of the Mysterious Soprano.
46.	11/ 9/1920	The Mysterious Bottle.
47.	18/ 9/1920	The Case of the Missing Patient.
48.	25/ 9/1920	The Purloined Pork.
49.	2/10/1920	The Case of the Bolshevik!
50.	9/10/1920	The Case of the Orator.
51.	16/10/1920	The Trunk Mystery.
52.	23/10/1920	The Disappearance of Dr Jotson.
53.	30/10/1920	The Case of the Boat Club.
54.	6/11/1920	The Case of the Gunpowder Plot.
55.	13/11/1920	The Case of the Lost Chord.
56.	20/11/1920	The Case of the Charlady.
57.	27/11/1920	The Case of the Corn-Plaster.
58.	4/12/1920	The Case of Podgers. M.P.
59.	11/12/1920	The Case of the Cubist.
60.	18/12/1920	The Case of the Dentist.
61.	25/12/1920	The Mystery of the Mince-Pie.
62.	1/ 1/1921	Pinkeye's New Year Resolution. By Dr. Jotson.

63. and 64. No Herlock Sholmes stories.

| 65. | 22/ 1/1921 | The Case of the Pink Rat. |

66. 67. & 68. No Herlock Sholmes stories.

| 69. | 19/ 2/1921 | The Case of the Lame Snail. |

Last story in paper.

HERLOCK SHOLMES stories in THE MAGNET.

469.	3/ 2/1917	The Case of his Lorship's Engagement.
471.	17/ 2/1917	The Missing Minister.
472.	24/ 2/1917	The Clue of the Chanting Cheese.
473.	3/ 3/1917	The Missing Moke.
474.	10/ 3/1917	The Vanished Aliens.
498.	25/ 8/1917	The Mystery of the Dustbin.
501.	15/ 9/1917	The Case of the American Clock.
505.	13/10/1917	The Case of the Hidden Hun.
506.	20/10/1917	The Secretary's Double.
508.	3/11/1917	The Lottery-Ticket.
520.	26/ 1/1918	Herlock Sholmes at Monte Carlo.

HERLOCK SHOLMES stories in THE MAGNET. (cont.)

521.	2/ 2/1918	The Case of the Financier.
551.	31/ 8/1918	The Case of the Missing Wife.
564.	30/11/1918	The Case of the Missing M.S.
		By Monty Lowther.
690.	30/ 4/1921	The Case of the Lost Sapphire.
		By Dr Jotson.
691.	7/ 5/1921	The Case of the Haunted Coal Shed.
		By Dr Jotson.
700.	9/ 7/1921	The Case of the Lost Nugget.
		By Dr Jotson.
723.	17/12/1921	That Ghostly Xmas Knight.
		By Dr Jotson.
727.	14/ 1/1922	The Lost Persian. By Dr Jotson.

SHEERLUCK JONES stories in THE MAGNET.
(with Dr Spotson)

1651.	7/10/1939	The Disappearance of Dunn Brown.
		By Hector Hutt.
1659.	2/12/1939	Bagging the Bombster.
		By Hector Hutt.
1660.	9/12/1939	Jones — The Master Spy!
		By Hector Hutt.
1664.	6/ 1/1940	The Ruffstuff Rhythm Boys.
		By Hector Hutt.

TOM MERRY'S OWN ANNUAL —
featuring HERLOCK SHOLMES.

No. 2.	1950	The Missing Millionaire
No. 4.	1952	The Case of the Perplexed Painter.

Stories of HERLOCK SHOLMES in the
GEM Library.

479.	14/ 4/1917	The Red Tape Mystery.
482.	5/ 5/1917	The Case of the Escaped Hun.
483.	12/ 5/1917	The Case of the Current Bun.
485.	26/ 5/1917	The Case of the Russian Revolution.
486.	2/ 6/1917	The Last of the Potatoes.
488.	16/ 6/1917	On the Scent.
490.	30/ 6/1917	The Case of the Teuton's Trousers.

Stories of HERLOCK SHOLMES in the
GEM Library (cont.)

493	21/ 7/1917	The Missing Margarine.
526.	9/ 3/1918	A Murder Mystery.

HERLOCK SHOLMES stories in
THE PENNY POPULAR.

114.	26/ 3/1921	The Case of the Potato Jacket.
118.	23/ 4/1921	The Mystery of the Vacant House. By Dr Jotson.
288.	26/ 7/1924	The Schwottem Ray.
290.	9/ 8/1924	The Mystery of the Green Crab.
292.	23/ 8/1924	The Golden Cow.
294.	6/ 9/1924	The White Rabbit.
296.	30/ 9/1924	The Unguarded Goal.
298.	4/10/1924	The Mystery of Moldy Manor.
302.	1/11/1924	The Silver Wishbone.
310.	27/12/1924	The Secret in the Pudding Bag.

INDEX